Lecture Notes in Computer Science 8715

Commenced Publication in 1973
Founding and Former Series Editors:
Gerhard Goos, Juris Hartmanis, and Jan van Leeuwen

Magnus Jonsson   Alexey Vinel
Boris Bellalta   Evgeny Belyaev (Eds.)

Multiple Access Communications

7th International Workshop, MACOM 2014
Halmstad, Sweden, August 27-28, 2014
Proceedings

 Springer

Volume Editors

Magnus Jonsson
Alexey Vinel
Halmstad University
School of Information Science, Computer and Electrical Engineering
Kristian IV:s väg 3, 30118 Halmstad, Sweden
E-mail: {magnus.jonsson, alexey.vinel}@hh.se

Boris Bellalta
Universitat Pompeu Fabra
Department of Information and Communication Technologies
Roc Boronat 138, 08018 Barcelona, Spain
E-mail: boris.bellalta@upf.edu

Evgeny Belyaev
Tampere University of Technology
Department of Signal Processing
Korkeakoulunkatu 3, 33720 Tampere, Finland
E-mail: evgeny.belyaev@tut.fi

ISSN 0302-9743   e-ISSN 1611-3349
ISBN 978-3-319-10261-0   e-ISBN 978-3-319-10262-7
DOI 10.1007/978-3-319-10262-7
Springer Cham Heidelberg New York Dordrecht London

Library of Congress Control Number: 2014946081

LNCS Sublibrary: SL 5 – Computer Communication Networks and Telecommunications

Typesetting: Camera-ready by author, data conversion by Scientific Publishing Services, Chennai, India

Printed on acid-free paper

Springer is part of Springer Science+Business Media (www.springer.com)

Preface

It is our great pleasure to present the proceedings of the 7th International Workshop on Multiple Access Communications (MACOM) that was held in Halmstad during August 27–28, 2014. Previous editions were organized in Vilnius (2013), Maynooth (2012), Trento (2011), Barcelona (2010), Dresden (2009), and Saint-Petersburg (2008).

Our gratitude goes to the Technical Program Committee and external reviewers for their efforts in selecting 12 high-quality contributions (out of 22 submitted) to be presented and discussed in the workshop.

The contributions gathered in these proceedings describe the latest advancements in the field of multiple access communications, with an emphasis on reliability issues, physical layer techniques, cognitive radio, medium access control protocols, and video coding.

Finally, we would like to take this opportunity to express our gratitude to all the participants, together with the local organizers, who helped to make MACOM 2014 a very successful event.

August 2014

Magnus Jonsson
Boris Bellalta
Evgeny Belyaev
Alexey Vinel

Organization

MACOM 2014 was organized by Halmstad University, Sweden.

Executive Committee

General Co-chairs

Magnus Jonsson	HH, Sweden
Alexey Vinel	HH, Sweden

TPC Co-chairs

Boris Bellalta	UPF, Spain
Evgeny Belyaev	TUT, Finland

Local Chair

Eva Nestius	HH, Halmstad

Publicity and Web Chair

Jaume Barcelo	UPF, Spain

Publication Chair

Nikita Lyamin	HH, Sweden

Technical Program Committee

Konstantin Avrachenkov	Inria Sophia Antipolis, France
Florin Avram	Université de Pau, France
Abdelmalik Bachir	Imperial College London, UK
Sandjai Bhulai	VU University Amsterdam, The Netherlands
Giuseppe Bianchi	University of Rome Tor Vergata, Italy
Torsten Braun	University of Bern, Switzerland
Raffaele Bruno	IIT-CNR, Italy
Peter Buchholz	TU Dortmund, Germany
Claudia Campolo	University Mediterranea of Reggio Calabria, Italy
Cristina Cano	Hamilton Institute, Ireland
Eduardo Cerqueira	UCLA, USA
Periklis Chatzimisios	Alexander TEI of Thessaloniki, Greece

Young-June Choi	Ajou University, South Korea
Tugrul Dayar	Bilkent University, Turkey
Javier Del Ser	TECNALIA, Spain
Desislava Dimitrova	University of Bern, Switzerland
Alexander Dudin	Belarusian State University, Belarus
Marc Emmelmann	Fraunhofer FOKUS, Germany
Lorenzo Favalli	University of Pavia, Italy
Dieter Fiems	Ghent University, Belgium
Andres Garcia-Saavedra	National University of Ireland Maynooth, Ireland
Marco Gramaglia	Istituto Superiore Mario Boella, Italy
Geert Heijenk	University of Twente, The Netherlands
Andras Horvath	University of Turin, Italy
Ganguk Hwang	KAIST, South Korea
Dragi Kimovski	University for Information Science and Technology, Macedonia
Valentina Klimenok	Belarusian State University, Belarus
Jarkko Kneckt	Nokia Reseach Center, Finland
Vinay Kolar	IBM Research, India
Kristina Kunert	Halmstad University, Sweden
Douglas Leith	Hamilton Institute, Ireland
Matthias Lott	DOCOMO Communications Laboratories Europe GmbH, Germany
David Malone	Hamilton Institute, Ireland
Vincenzo Mancuso	IMDEA Networks Institute, Spain
Arturas Medeisis	Vilnius Gediminas Technical University, Lithuania
Michela Meo	Politecnico di Torino, Italy
Enzo Mingozzi	University of Pisa, Italy
Edmundo Monteiro	University of Coimbra, Portugal
David Morales	Hong Kong University of Science and Technology, SAR China
Dmitry Osipov	IITP RAS, Russia
Evgeny Osipov	LTU Luleå University of Technology, Sweden
Alexander Pechinkin	Institute of Informatics Problems, RAS, Russia
Edison Pignaton de Freitas	Federal University of Santa Maria, Brazil
Vicent Pla	Universitat Politecnica de Valencia, Spain
Zsolt Saffer	Budapest University of Technology and Economics, Hungary
Nikos Sagias	University of the Peloponnese, Greece
Pablo Salvador	IMDEA Networks Institute, Spain
Bruno Sericola	Inria Rennes - Bretagne Atlantique, France
Susanna Spinsante	Università Politecnica delle Marche, Italy
Andrey Trofimov	Saint-Petersburg State University of Aerospace Instrumentation, Russia

Mikko Valkama   Tampere University of Technology, Finland
Rob van der Mei   Centrum voor Wiskunde en Informatica,
                                   The Netherlands
Bernhard Walke   RWTH Aachen University, Germany
Till Wollenberg   University of Rostock, Germany
Yan Zhang   Simula Research Laboratory and University of
                                   Oslo, Norway

Table of Contents

Signal Processing

Digital Phase Updating Loop and Delay-Doppler Space Division Multiplexing for Higher Order MPSK*

Yutaka Jitsumatsu and Tohru Kohda

Dept. Informatics, Kyushu University
744 Motooka, Nishi-ku, Fukuoka, 819-0395, Japan
{jitumatu,kohda}@inf.kyushu-u.ac.jp

Abstract. An alternative to the use of higher order Quadrature Amplitude Modulation (QAM) that shows strong variations of output amplitude is the use of higher order Phase Shift Keying (PSK). The bit error probability of higher order PSK is sensitive to phase distortion that is caused by propagation delay and Doppler frequency estimation errors. Phase Updating Loop (PUL) is a generalization of a Phase Locked Loop (PLL) that can estimate the delay and the Doppler accurately. In order to realize a higher order PSK, we recently proposed a delay-Doppler Space Division Multiplexing (dD-SDM) method in which a parameter space consisting of delay and Doppler is partitioned into several subspaces and each subspace has its assigned signature codes. In this paper, digital PUL is defined. Simulation results show that by the use of the dD-SDM method together with digital PUL we can successfully demodulate 256PSK data.

Keywords: Spread Spectrum Multiple Access, Code Division Multiple Access, multi-path detection, delay-Doppler determination.

1 Introduction

Time and frequency synchronization error causes a phase distortion as well as inter-symbol interference and inter-carrier interference in multi-carrier communications [1]. Estimation of the propagation delay and Doppler frequency is a classical problem in radar [2–4]. The time and frequency synchronization process is normally separated into two steps: initial acquisition in which course alignment of time and frequency is achieved, followed by tracking in which minimization of synchronization error is performed [1].

We proposed a Phase Updating Loop (PUL) method for a Gabor Division/Spread Spectrum System (GD/S³) that can detect the delay and Doppler of a channel individually and cooperatively [5]. One of the important features of PUL is that it can perform both acquisition and tracking.

---

* This research is supported by the Aihara Project, the FIRST program from JSPS, initiated by CSTP and JSPS KAKENHI Grant Number 25820162.

M. Jonsson et al. (Eds.): MACOM 2014, LNCS 8715, pp. 1–15, 2014.

As an application of PUL, a multi-target detection method, called Code Division Multiple Targets(CDMT), has been recently proposed [7,8]. A target space, which is a range of allowable delay and Doppler, is divided into several disjoint spaces and each sub-space has its associated two-dimensional (2D) Spread Spectrum (SS) code. Then, multiple delay-Doppler (d-D) targets are resolved by the CDMT technique. This implies that d-D space can be used as a fourth axis for multiplexing, in addition to the conventional time, frequency, and code axes. This motivated us to propose a delay-Doppler Space Division Multiplexing (dD-SDM) [9] in which parallel data are transmitted through d-D sub-spaces.

It is well-known that higher order Quadrature Amplitude Modulation (QAM) signals show strong variations of output amplitude and have large peak-to-average power ratio (PAPR). Then, linearity is required for amplifiers in the transceivers, which leads to high power consumption. An alternative is the use of higher order multiple phase shift keying (MPSK) [10]. A promising application for such higher order MPSK is optical communications [11–13].

Using dD-SDM we have recently shown that 16PSK data is easily demodulated [9]. In this paper, digital PUL is defined. Simulation results show that 256PSK data can be demodulated by using dD-SDM together with digital PUL. The list of abbreviations used in this paper is shown in Table 1.

Table 1. List of Abbreviations

PUL	Phase Updating Loop
dD-SDM	Delay-Doppler Space Division Multiplexing
GD/S^3	Gabor Division/Spread Spectrum System
CDMT	Code Division Multiple Target
TD	Time Domain
FD	Frequency Domain
TFS	Time Frequency Symmetry

2   Discrete-Time Phase Updating Loop

A PUL receiver utilizes time domain (TD) and frequency domain (FD) correlators that are defined in continuous-time and continuous-frequency domains, respectively. In this paper, a discrete-time and discrete-frequency version of the PUL receiver is defined. The reasons why we introduce this discrete-time and discrete-frequency version of the PUL receiver are two-fold: First, an FD correlator needs an FD expression of the received signal, which is usually processed in a digital domain, i.e., it is obtained by Discrete Fourier Transform (DFT). Second, it was suggested in [8] that TD and FD correlator outputs can be calculated by the Fourier Transform (FT) of a product of the received signal and TD templates and by the inverse FT of a product of FT of the received signal and TD templates.

A received signal in a narrow band model of a channel with a delay t_d and a Doppler f_D is defined by [14]

$$r(t) = \alpha s(t - t_d)e^{j\{2\pi f_D(t - \frac{t_d}{2}) + \varphi\}} + \eta(t), \tag{1}$$

where $s(t)$ is a tramsmitted signal, $\eta(t)$ is an additive white Gaussian noise (AWGN), and $\mathbf{j}$ is an imaginary unit. In this paper, a discrete time and discrete frequency version of (1) is considered. Let T_s be a sampling interval and a homodyne receiver shown in Fig. 1 is assumed, but the following discussion is also valid for heterodyne receivers. The L-point DFT is used to obtain an FD signal. Then, the frequency gap between two adjacent frequency bins in the FD signal is $F_s = 1/(LT_s)$. We use ℓ and k for time and frequency variables.

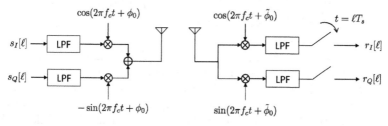

Fig. 1. A homodyne receiver, where f_c, ϕ_0, and $\tilde{\phi}_0$ are the carrier frequency, an initial phase of the carrier waveform, and an inital phase phase of a local oscillator. LPF stands for low-pass filter.

A complex-valued baseband signal is expressed by $s[\ell] = s_I[\ell] + \mathbf{j}s_Q[\ell]$ in the discrete-time domain, which is passed through a low-pass filter, modulated with in-phase and quadrature-phase carrier signals, and then transmitted. A channel should have a propagation delay and a Doppler shift. Suppose the delay and Doppler of the channel are given by $t_d = \ell_d T_s$ and $f_D = k_D F_s$. A discrete-time received signal can be modelled as (See Fig.1)

$$r[\ell] = r_I[\ell] + \mathbf{j}r_Q[\ell] = \alpha s[\ell - \ell_d]W_L^{-k_D(\ell - \frac{\ell_d}{2}) - \beta_0} + \eta[\ell], \tag{2}$$

where ℓ_d, k_D, $W_L = e^{-\mathbf{j}2\pi/L}$, α, $\beta_0 \in \{0, 1, L - 1\}$, and $\eta[\ell]$ are a normalized delay, a normalized Doppler, twiddle factor, an attenuation factor, an initial phase, and a noise process.

It should be noted that sampling frequency $1/T_s$ should be higher than the Nyquist rate of the maximum frequency of the received signal, which is the bandwidth of the transmitted signal plus the Doppler shift. The continuous Doppler frequency can be expressed by $f_D = (k_D + \epsilon)F_s$ with $|\epsilon| < 1/2$. The samples L should be large so that $F_s = 1/(LT_s)$ is small enough to realise high frequency resolution. It is well-known that the received signal is degraded if $|\epsilon| \approx 1/2$. This phenomenon is referred to as scalloping loss [15]. Such a loss can be avoided by windowing or increasing L with zero-padding.

A time shift of $-\frac{\ell_d}{2}$ in the exponent of Eq.(2) is introduced so that $r[\ell]$ and its DFT, $R[k]$, are perfectly symmetrical in terms of ℓ_d and k_D. Such a signal is said to satisfy Time Frequency Symmetry (TFS) [5]. Determination of delay and Doppler is a classical problem in radar and sonar [2, 3]. The compressed sensing technique has been recently applied to radar [16, 17]. An advantage of compressed sensing-based radar is that multiple targets can be identified with improved resolution.

Let $v^{\mathrm{GD}}[\ell; \mathcal{X}]$ be a signature waveform, defined by

$$v^{\mathrm{GD}}[\ell; \mathcal{X}] = \frac{1}{\sqrt{NN'}} \sum_{m=1}^{N} \sum_{m'=1}^{N'} X_{mm'}^{\mathrm{GD}} z[\ell - mM] W_L^{m'M'(\ell - \frac{mM}{2})} \qquad (3)$$

where $M = T_c/T_s$, $M' = F_c/F_s$, $z[\ell]$, and $\mathcal{X} = \{X_{mm'}^{\mathrm{GD}}\}$ are a normalized chip duration, a normalized chip frequency, a Gaussian chip waveform, and a 2D SS code[1] with a chip address (m, m'), where T_c and F_c are the chip duration and chip frequency. A time shift of $-\frac{mM}{2}$ in the exponent of Eq.(3) is introduced so that $v^{\mathrm{GD}}[\ell]$ and its FT, $V^{\mathrm{GD}}[k]$ satisfy TFS. Then, a transmitted signal for a GD/S^3 is defined by

$$s[\ell] = \sum_{q=1}^{P} \sum_{q'=1}^{P'} d_q v^{\mathrm{GD}}[\ell - qNM; \mathcal{X}] W_L^{-q'N'M'(\ell - \frac{qNM}{2})} \qquad (4)$$

where d_q, N, N', P, and P' are a data symbol with a data address $q = (q, q')$, a TD spreading factor, an FD spreading factor, and the number of data in the time and frequency domains.

An important feature of a GD/S^3 receiver is that it employs two types of correlators. One estimates Doppler and the other estimates delay. GD/S^3 employs TD and FD integrators alternately. We first proposed FD coded TD integrators for detecting Doppler and TD coded FD integrators for detecting delay. Such a pair of integrators is referred to as an *original pair*. Exchanging the role of TD and FD codes, we then proposed a TD-coded TD integrator for detecting Doppler and an FD-coded FD integrator for detecting delay. Such a pair of integrators is called a *complementary pair*. The original and complementary pairs work in high and low SNR environments, respectively, as shown below.

---

[1] In the previous papers [5–9], separable codes, i.e., $X_{m,m'}^{\mathrm{GD}} = X_m \cdot X_{m'}'$ are used. A more general case of both separable and nonseparable codes is treated in this paper.

Let us concentrate on the original pair of TD and FD integrators. The outputs of N FD-coded TD integrators and N' TD-coded FD integrators are

$$
\begin{aligned}
c_{\boldsymbol{p},n}^{\mathrm{GD(FD)}}[\mu;\hat{\ell}_d] =& T_s \sum_{\ell=0}^{L-1} r[\ell]\bar{u}_n^{\mathrm{FD}}[\ell-nM-pNM-\hat{\ell}_d;\mathcal{Y}] \\
& \times W_L^{(p'N'M'+\mu)(\ell-\frac{\ell M+pNM+\hat{\ell}_d}{2})} W_L^{\overline{\varphi}_{\mathrm{orig}}^{\mathrm{GD(FD)}}(\hat{\ell}_d,\mu)},
\end{aligned}
\tag{5}
$$

$$
\begin{aligned}
C_{\boldsymbol{p},n'}^{\mathrm{GD(TD)}}[\sigma;\hat{k}_D] =& F_s \sum_{k=0}^{L-1} R[k]\bar{U}_{n'}^{\mathrm{TD}}[k-n'M'-p'N'M'-\hat{k}_D;\mathcal{Y}] \\
& \times W_L^{-(pNM+\sigma)(k-\frac{kM'+p'N'M'+\hat{k}_D}{2})} W_L^{-\overline{\varphi}_{\mathrm{orig}}^{\mathrm{GD(TD)}}(\sigma,\hat{k}_D)}
\end{aligned}
\tag{6}
$$

for $n=1,2,\ldots,N$ and $n'=1,2,\ldots,N'$, where $R[k]$ is the L-point discrete Fourier transform of $r[\ell]$, μ and σ are controlled parameters for detecting k_D and ℓ_d, respectively, $\hat{k}_D$ and $\hat{\ell}_d$ are prescribed values, $\mathcal{Y}$ is a 2D SS code for guessing $\mathcal{X}$, and

$$
u_n^{\mathrm{FD}}[\ell;\mathcal{Y}] = \frac{1}{\sqrt{N'}} \sum_{n'=0}^{N'-1} Y_{nn'}^{\mathrm{GD}} z[\ell] W_L^{-n'M'(\ell+\frac{nM}{2})},
\tag{7}
$$

$$
U_{n'}^{\mathrm{TD}}[k;\mathcal{Y}] = \frac{1}{\sqrt{N}} \sum_{n=0}^{N-1} Y_{nn'}^{\mathrm{GD}} Z[k] W_L^{nN(k+\frac{n'M'}{2})}
\tag{8}
$$

are an FD coded TD template and a TD coded FD template, respectively, and $\overline{\varphi}_{\mathrm{orig}}^{\mathrm{GD(TD)}}(\hat{\ell}_d,\mu)$ and $\overline{\varphi}_{\mathrm{orig}}^{\mathrm{GD(FD)}}(\sigma,\hat{k}_D)$ are the phase shift caused by compositions of two time-frequency shifts [8] (See Appendix).

TD and FD integrators are designed so that t_d and f_D can be estimated separately. Note the TD and FD templates are decompositions of $v^{\mathrm{GD}}[\ell;\mathcal{X}] = \frac{1}{\sqrt{N}}\sum_{n=0}^{N-1} u_n^{\mathrm{FD}}[\ell-nM;\mathcal{X}]$ and its FT $V^{\mathrm{GD}}[k;\mathcal{X}] = \frac{1}{\sqrt{N'}}\sum_{n'=0}^{N'-1} U_{n'}^{\mathrm{TD}}[k-n'M';\mathcal{X}]$.

The real parts of Eq.(5) and (6) are evaluated as follows: Assume $\mathcal{Y}=\mathcal{X}$, $q=p$, and $d_p=1$. A simple trigonometric $\frac{1}{N}\sum_{i=1}^{N} z^i = \frac{1}{N}\frac{1-z}{z(1-z^N)} = e^{j\pi(N+1)x}\frac{\sin N\pi x}{N\sin\pi x} \approx e^{j\pi(N+1)x}\mathrm{sinc}(Nx)$ for $|x|<1$, $N\gg1$ and $z=e^{j2\pi x}$, where $\mathrm{sinc}(x)=\sin\pi x/(\pi x)$, gives

$$
\begin{aligned}
\Re\left\{c_{\boldsymbol{p},n}^{\mathrm{GD(FD)}}[\mu;\hat{\ell}_d]\right\} =& \frac{\alpha}{\sqrt{N}}\tilde{\theta}_{zz}[\hat{\ell}_d-\ell_d,\mu-k_D]\cdot\mathrm{sinc}(N'M'(\hat{\ell}_d-\ell_d)/L) \\
& \cdot\cos(\tfrac{2\pi}{L}\{\beta_0+\bar{\delta}(\hat{\ell}_d,\mu)|_{q=p}+\tfrac{N'+1}{2}M'(\hat{\ell}_d-\ell_d)-nM(\mu-k_D)\}),
\end{aligned}
\tag{9}
$$

$$
\begin{aligned}
\Re\left\{C_{\boldsymbol{p},n'}^{\mathrm{GD(TD)}}[\sigma;\hat{k}_D]\right\} =& \frac{\alpha}{\sqrt{N'}}\tilde{\theta}_{ZZ}[\hat{k}_D-k_D,-(\sigma-\ell_d)]\cdot\mathrm{sinc}(NM(\hat{k}_D-k_D)/L) \\
& \cdot\cos(\tfrac{2\pi}{L}\{\beta_0+\bar{\Delta}(\sigma,\hat{k}_D)|_{q=p}+n'M'(\sigma-\ell_d)-\tfrac{N+1}{2}M(\hat{k}_D-k_D)\}),
\end{aligned}
\tag{10}
$$

where $\tilde{\theta}_{xy}[\tau,\nu] = \frac{1}{\sqrt{L}}\sum_{\ell=0}^{L-1}x[\ell]\bar{y}[\ell-\tau]W_L^{\nu(\ell-\tau/2)}$ and $\tilde{\theta}_{XY}[\nu,-\tau] = \frac{1}{\sqrt{L}}\sum_{k=0}^{L-1}X[k]\bar{Y}[k-\nu]W_L^{-\tau(k-\nu/2)}$ are discrete-time discrete-frequency version of ambiguity function and $\Re\{z\}$ denotes the real part of z. See the Appendix for $\bar{\delta}(\hat{\ell}_d, \mu)$ and $\bar{\Delta}(\sigma, \hat{k}_D)$. The sinc functions in Eqs.(9) and (10) come from summations in the correlator outputs with respect to the FD and TD codes. The phase terms that are proportional to $(N + 1)T_c$ and $(N' + 1)F_c$ in (9) and (10) also come from the summations with respect to the FD and TD codes. Because sinc(x) takes large values when $|x| < 1$, $|\hat{\ell}_d - \ell_d| < 1/(N'M')$ and $|\hat{k}_D - k_D| < 1/(NM)$ are necessary for Eqs.(9) and (10) to have peak values. Namely, the prescribed values for $\hat{\ell}_d$ and $\hat{k}_D$ must be very close to ℓ_d and k_D. The Gaussian ambiguity functions in Eqs.(9) and (10) imply that $|\mu - k_D| < 3\sigma_f$ and $|\sigma - \ell_d| < 3\sigma_t$ are necessary for such integrator outputs to have peak values, where σ_t and σ_f are the standard deviations of a Gaussian waveform in TD and FD, i.e., $\sigma_t^2 = \sum_\ell \ell^2 z[\ell]$ and $\sigma_f^2 = \sum_k k^2 Z[k]$. Hence, σ and μ are not extremely accurate. This situation implies that the original pair of TD and FD integrators work for a high SNR. On the other hand, a complementary pair of integrators work for a low SNR (See Appendix).

A passive PUL for an original pair of integrators updates $(\hat{\ell}_{d,s}, \hat{k}_{D,s})$ as

$$\hat{\ell}_{d,s} = \sigma_* \text{ if } s \text{ is odd}, \quad \hat{k}_{D,s} = \mu_* \text{ if } s \text{ is even}, \tag{11}$$

where

$$(\sigma_*, n'_*) = \arg \max_{\sigma, n'} \Re \left\{ C_{p,n'}^{\mathrm{GD(TD)}}[\sigma; \hat{k}_{D,s-1}] \right\}, \tag{12}$$

$$(\mu_*, n_*) = \arg \max_{\mu, n} \Re \left\{ c_{p,n}^{\mathrm{GD(FD)}}[\mu; \hat{\ell}_{d,s-1}] \right\}. \tag{13}$$

The initial value $(\ell_{d,0}, k_{D,0})$ is chosen arbitrarily. One may choose $(\ell_{d,0}, k_{D,0}) = (0, 0)$.

3   Active PUL

By substituting (4) into (2), we obtain the received signal for a passive PUL as

$$r[\ell] = \alpha W_L^{-\beta_0} \sum_{q=1}^{P} \sum_{q'=1}^{P'} d_q W_L^{-\bar{\phi}(pNM, p'N'M'; \ell_d, k_D)} v^{\mathrm{GD}}[\ell - qNM - \ell_d; \mathcal{X}]$$

$$\cdot W_L^{-(q'N'M' + k_D)(\ell - \frac{qNM + \ell_d}{2})}, \tag{14}$$

where $\bar{\phi}(qNM, q'N'M'; \ell_d, k_D) = \frac{1}{2} \begin{vmatrix} qNM & q'N'M' \\ \ell_d & k_D \end{vmatrix}$ is a phase distortion. This should be compensated for at a receiver or transmitter, because it increases as q and q' increase. Phase compensation methods for the receiver and transmitter, called passive and active PULs, have been proposed [5]. For a passive PUL, $\bar{\phi}(qNM, q'N'M'; \ell_d, k_D)$ is compensated for by $\overline{\varphi}_{\mathrm{orig}}^{\mathrm{GD(FD)}}$ and $\overline{\varphi}_{\mathrm{orig}}^{\mathrm{GD(TD)}}$.

A receiver with passive PUL updates the estimated delay and Doppler, as shown in (12) and (13). Such estimated values can be fed back to the transmitter,

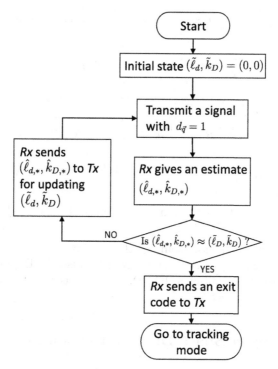

Fig. 2. A flowchart of a procedure of active PUL

which then updates its transmitted signal so that time and frequency offsets as well as phase distortion are compensated for at the transmitter. Consider a communication system consisting of a transmitter, a receiver, a feedforward channel, and a feedback channel through which the estimated delay and Doppler are informed. Such a system is called an active PUL.

Let $(\widetilde{\ell}_d, \widetilde{k}_D)$ and $(\hat{\ell}_d, \hat{k}_D)$ be estimations for the (ℓ_d, k_D) used in a transmitter and a receiver, respectively. See Fig. 2 for the procedure of an active PUL. A passive PUL updates $(\hat{\ell}_d, \hat{k}_D)$ within the receiver, hence the update process is done quickly, while it may take a long time to feedback the estimated values of delay and Doppler. Hence, it is reasonable to suppose that $(\widetilde{\ell}_d, \widetilde{k}_D)$ and $(\hat{\ell}_d, \hat{k}_D)$ are different in general. We further assume that the transmitter knows only the former, while the receiver knows both $(\widetilde{\ell}_d, \widetilde{k}_D)$ and $(\hat{\ell}_d, \hat{k}_D)$. For an active PUL, the transmitted signal in (4) is replaced by

$$\widetilde{s}[\ell] = \sum_{q=1}^{P} \sum_{q'=1}^{P'} d_q W_L^{\bar{\phi}(qNM, q'N'M'; \widetilde{\ell}_d, \widetilde{k}_D)} v^{\mathrm{GD}}[\ell - qNM + \widetilde{\ell}_d; \mathcal{X}]$$

$$\cdot W_L^{-(q'N'M' - \widetilde{k}_D)(\ell - \frac{qNM - \widetilde{\ell}_d}{2})}. \tag{15}$$

The phase distortion $\bar{\phi}(qNM, q'NM; \ell_d, k_D)$ in (14) is compensated for at the transmitter if $\widetilde{\ell}_d$ and $\widetilde{k}_D$ are sufficiently close to the actual delay and Doppler.

Let $\tilde{r}[\ell]$ and $\tilde{R}[k]$ be a received signal associated with (15) and its FT. Then, the TD and FD correlator outputs for an active PUL are

$$c_{\boldsymbol{p},n,\mathrm{Act}}^{\mathrm{GD(FD)}}[\mu; \hat{\ell}_d] = T_s \sum_{\ell} \tilde{r}[\ell] \overline{u}_n^{\mathrm{FD}}[\ell - nM - pNM - \hat{\ell}_d + \tilde{\ell}_d; \mathcal{Y}]$$

$$\cdot W_L^{\{(p'N'M' + \mu - \tilde{k}_D)(n - \frac{nM + pNM + \hat{n}_d - \tilde{\ell}_d}{2}) + \overline{\varphi}_{\mathrm{orig,Act}}^{\mathrm{GD(FD)}}(\hat{\ell}_d, \mu)\}}, \qquad (16)$$

$$C_{\boldsymbol{p},n',\mathrm{Act}}^{\mathrm{GD(TD)}}[\sigma; \hat{f}_D] = F_s \sum_{k} \tilde{R}[k] \overline{U}_{i'}^{\mathrm{TD}}[k - n'M' - p'N'M' - \hat{k}_D + \tilde{k}_D; \mathcal{Y}]$$

$$\cdot W_L^{\{(pNM + \sigma - \tilde{\ell}_d)(k - \frac{n'M' + p'N'M' + \hat{k}_D - \tilde{k}_D}{2}) + \overline{\varphi}_{\mathrm{orig,Act}}^{\mathrm{GD(TD)}}(\sigma, \hat{k}_D)\}}. \qquad (17)$$

See the Appendix for the definition of the phase terms $\overline{\varphi}_{\mathrm{orig,Act}}^{\mathrm{GD(FD)}}(\hat{\ell}_d, \mu)$ and $\overline{\varphi}_{\mathrm{orig,Act}}^{\mathrm{GD(TD)}}(\sigma, \hat{k}_D)$.

An active PUL system is more complex than passive PUL. A benefit of active PUL is that we can suppress an excess bandwidth caused by Doppler shift. More importantly, active PUL realizes a dD-SDM that leads to higher order MPSK, as explained in the next section.

4   Delay Doppler Space Division Multiplexing

Multiple pairs of delay and Doppler (d-D) can be resolved by the CDMT technique [7,8] in which a d-D target space is partitioned into several sub-spaces (See Fig. 3 (a)) and each sub-space has its associated 2D SS code. This implies that we may transmit one data through each path. To do this, we introduce artificial delays and Dopplers, denoted by $(\ell_{d,i}^*, k_{D,i}^*)$, which are allocated in the center of each target sub-space, where i is the subspace number.

The system defined below is called dD-SDM [9]. Fig. 3 shows that dD-SDM is realized by the use of a delay-Doppler space. Space Division Multiplexing (SDM) is employed in optical fiber communication [12,13], where the 'space' means distinct fibers. Multiple-Input Multiple-Output (MIMO) communication is an example of SDM, where 'space' means physical transmitters or receivers.

Let $d_q^{\mathrm{GD}} = W_{\mathcal{M}}^{-(m_q-1)}$ for $m_q = 1, 2, \ldots, \mathcal{M}$, where $W_{\mathcal{M}} = e^{-\mathrm{j}\frac{2\pi}{\mathcal{M}}}$ is a twiddle factor. Suppose time-frequency synchronization is already acquired within $\frac{T_c}{2}$ and $\frac{F_c}{2}$ by PUL. Phase-tuned layers can easily realize 8PSK, while sidelobes are observed in the outputs of phase-tuned layers for 16PSK [6]. Hence, we choose 8PSK as a basic component for modulation.

An artificial delay-Doppler $(\ell_{d,i}^*, k_{D,i}^*)$ is introduced to the transmitted signal. Then, Eq.(4) is replaced by

$$s^{\mathrm{SDM}}[\ell] = \sum_{q} d_q^{\mathrm{GD}} v^{\mathrm{GD}}[\ell - qNM - \ell_{d,i}^*; \mathcal{X}^{(i)}]$$

$$\times W_L^{-(q'N'M' + k_{D,i}^*)(\ell - \frac{qNM + \ell_{d,i}^*}{2})}, \qquad (18)$$

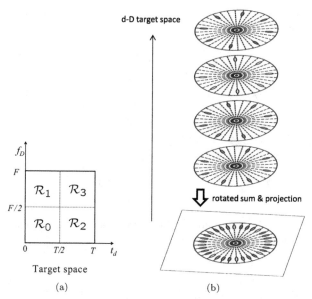

d-D target space

rotated sum & projection

Target space

$\mathcal{R}_1$ | $\mathcal{R}_3$

$\mathcal{R}_0$ | $\mathcal{R}_2$

(a)   (b)

Fig. 3. Delay-Doppler space division multiplexing. (a) A target space $[0, T] \times [0, F]$ is partitioned into $\mathcal{M}/8$ sub-spaces. (b) $\mathcal{M}/8$ rotated 8PSK data outputs are summed and projected onto the delay-Doppler space. Here, $\mathcal{M}$ is 32.

where $i = (m_q - 1) \bmod M/8$. Let $r^{\mathrm{SDM}}[\ell]$ and $R^{\mathrm{SDM}}[k]$ be a received signal associated with (18) and its FT.

A complementary pair of TD and FD integrators that can work in a low SNR is considered hereafter. Outputs of such integrators in the λ_p -th layer with the j-th code are defined as

$$
c_{\boldsymbol{p},n',\lambda_{\boldsymbol{p}},j}^{\mathrm{SDM(TD)}}[\mu; k_{d,j}^*]\Big|_{\mu=k_{D,j}^*}
$$
$$
= W_8^{\lambda_{\boldsymbol{p}}-1} W_{\mathcal{M}}^j T_s \sum_\ell r^{\mathrm{SDM}}[\ell]\overline{u_{n'}^{\mathrm{TD}}[\ell - pNM - \ell_{d,j}^*; \boldsymbol{Y}^{(j)}]}
$$
$$
\times W_L^{((p'N'M'+n'M'+k_{D,j}^*)(\ell-\frac{pNM+\ell_{d,j}^*}{2})+\overline{\varphi}_{\mathrm{comp}}^{\mathrm{GD(TD)}}(\ell_{d,j}^*,k_{d,j}^*))}, \tag{19}
$$

$$
C_{\boldsymbol{p},n,\ell_{\boldsymbol{p}}',j}^{\mathrm{SDM(FD)}}[\sigma; k_{D,j}^*]\Big|_{\sigma=\ell_{d,j}^*}
$$
$$
= W_8^{\ell_{\boldsymbol{p}}'-1} W_{\mathcal{M}}^j F_s \sum_k R^{\mathrm{SDM}}[k]\overline{U_n^{\mathrm{FD}}[k - p'N'M' - k_{D,j}^*; \boldsymbol{Y}'^{(j)}]}
$$
$$
\cdot W_L^{-((pNM+nM+\ell_{d,j}^*)(k-\frac{p'N'M'+k_{D,j}^*}{2}+\overline{\varphi}_{\mathrm{comp}}^{\mathrm{GD(TD)}}(\ell_{d,j}^*,k_{D,j}^*))}, \tag{20}
$$

where $\lambda_{\boldsymbol{p}}, \lambda_{\boldsymbol{p}}' \in \{1, 2, \ldots, 8\}$. Fig. 4 shows the layer number λ_q and code number j for MPSK data symbol demodulation when $\mathcal{M} = 32$. Note that $\frac{\mathcal{M}}{8} \cdot 8 \cdot (N + N')$

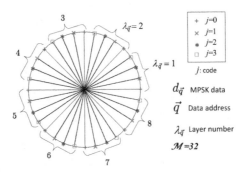

Fig. 4. Layer number and code number for MPSK data demodulation using phase-tuned layers and dD-SDM

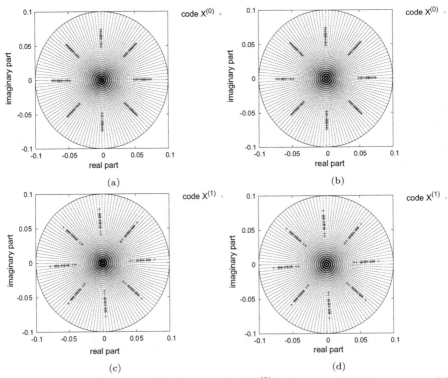

Fig. 5. (a) Demodulated 8PSK data signal of $\mathcal{X}^{(0)}$ before maximization process, (b) demodulated 8PSK data signal of $\mathcal{X}^{(0)}$ after maximization process, (c) demodulated 8PSK data signal of $\mathcal{X}^{(1)}$ before maximization process, and (d) demodulated 8PSK data signal of $\mathcal{X}^{(1)}$ after maximization process. $\mathcal{M} = 128$.

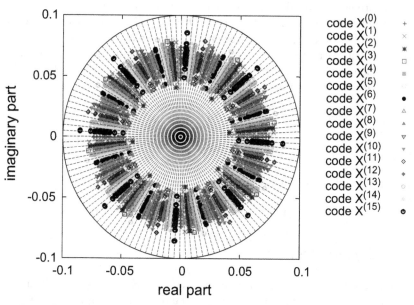

Fig. 6. Demodulated 128PSK data signals. The results of $(2\pi)/128$-shifted 8PSK data demoulation for 16 codes are combined.

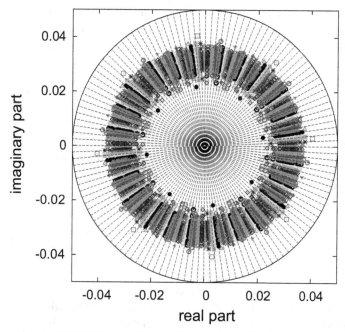

Fig. 7. Demodulated 256PSK data signals. The results of $(2\pi)/256$-shifted 8PSK data demoulation for 32 codes are combined.

correlators are used in total, that the noise and interference terms in the received signal in the layers are different from each other, and that the proposed receiver is expected to be robust to noise, interference, and synchronization errors. Then, real parts of the correlator outputs are used for demodulating the transmitted data. For each data address $\boldsymbol{p}$, $(n'_*, \lambda_{\boldsymbol{p},*}, j_*)$ and $(n_*, \lambda'_{\boldsymbol{p},*}, j'_*)$ of TD and FD correlators are determined as

$$(n'_*, \lambda_{\boldsymbol{p},*}, j_*) = \arg \max_{(n',\lambda,j)} \Re \left\{ c^{\text{SDM(TD)}}_{\boldsymbol{p},n',\lambda}[k^*_{D,j}; \ell^*_{d,j}] \right\}, \tag{21}$$

$$(n_*, \lambda'_{\boldsymbol{p},*}, j'_*) = \arg \max_{(n,\lambda',j')} \Re \left\{ C^{\text{SDM(FD)}}_{\boldsymbol{p},n,\lambda'}[\ell^*_{d,j'}; k^*_{D,j'}] \right\}. \tag{22}$$

Finally, data symbols are demodulated as

$$\hat{d}^{\text{SDM(TD)}}_{\boldsymbol{p}} = W_8^{\lambda_{\boldsymbol{p},*} - 1} W_{\mathcal{M}}^{j_*}, \quad \hat{d}^{\text{SDM(FD)}}_{\boldsymbol{p}} = W_8^{\lambda'_{\boldsymbol{p},*} - 1} W_{\mathcal{M}}^{j'_*}. \tag{23}$$

5   Simulation Results

We demonstrate constellations of demodulated MPSK data signals obtained by numerical simulation of a delay-Doppler space division multiplexing. In Fig. 5, MPSKdata with $\mathcal{M} = 128$ is demodulated, where $N = N' = 16$ SNR is 30dB and 16 codes are employed. We easily demodulate the 8PSK signal and $(2\pi)/128$ shifted 8PSK signal using codes $\mathcal{X}^{(0)}$ and $\mathcal{X}^{(1)}$, respectively. The maximization process in Eqs.(21) and (22) eliminate signals for other codes that are observed at the origin of graphs (a) and (c). Combining 16 constellations, we obtain Fig. 6. This situation is explained by Fig. 3. In Fig. 3, the number of codes is four and $\mathcal{M} = 8 \times 4 = 32$, while in Figs. 5 and 6 the number of codes is 16, the target space is divided into 4×4 sub-spaces, and $\mathcal{M} = 8 \times 16 = 128$. In Fig. 7, 256PSK is realized by combining 32 codes, where $N = N' = 32$ and SNR is 30dB. Note that the whole target space $[0, T] \times [0, F]$ is divided into $8 \times 4 = 32$ sub-spaces. The delay space is divided by 8 and the Doppler space is divided by 4. Note that the degree of freedom, or dimension, of the transmitted signal for dD-SDM is high. The dimension required to realize 256 PSK is $N \times N' = 1024$. In such an application for which available bandwidth is huge, the dD-SDM technique is promising because the demodulation of higher order PSK data is easy.

6   Concluding Remarks

This paper shows that we can easily demodulate 128PSK and 256PSK data by the use of a delay-Doppler space division multiplexing (dD-SDM) method. Discrete time and discrete frequency versions of passive and active PUL are defined. Note that the PAPRs of a transmitted signal in GD/S^3 is not small. A higher order PSK has an advantage in that we can reserve amplitude information about a transmitted signal to be used for channel estimation. This subject as well as bit error rate analysis and phase angle distribution of outputs in phase-tuned layers will be discussed in a separate paper.

References

1. Morelli, M., Kuo, C.-C.J., Pun, M.-O.: Synchronization techniques for orthogonal frequency division multiple access (OFDMA): A tutorial review. Proc. of the IEEE 95(7), 1394–1427 (2007)
2. Levanon, N., Mozeson, E.: Radar Signals. John Wiley & Sons (2004)
3. Woodward, P.M.: Probability and Information Theory, with Applications to Radar. McGraw-Hill, New York (1953)
4. Ville, J.: Théorie et applications de la notion de signal analytique. Câbles et Transmission (2), 61–74 (1948)
5. Kohda, T., Jitsumatsu, Y., Aihara, K.: Gabor division/spread spectrum system is separable in time and frequency synchronization. In: Proc. Veh. Technology Conf. 2013 Fall (2013)
6. Kohda, T., Jitsumatsu, Y., Aihara, K.: Recovering noncoherent MPSK signal with unknown delay and doppler using its ambiguity function. In: 4th Int. Workshop on Recent Advances in Broadband Access Networks (RABAN 2013), pp. 251–256 (2013)
7. Kohda, T., Jitsumatsu, Y., Aihara, K.: PLL-free receiver for Gabor division/spread spectrum system. In: Proc. 9th IEEE Int. Conf. Wireless and Mobile Computing, Networking and Commun. (WiMob 2013), pp. 662–669 (2013)
8. Jitsumatsu, Y., Kohda, T., Aihara, K.: Delay-doppler space division-based multiple-access solves multiple-target detection. In: Jonsson, M., Vinel, A., Bellalta, B., Marina, N., Dimitrova, D., Fiems, D. (eds.) MACOM 2013. LNCS, vol. 8310, pp. 39–53. Springer, Heidelberg (2013)
9. Kohda, T., Jitsumatsu, Y., Aihara, K.: Phase-tuned layers with multiple 2D SS codes realize 16PSK communication. In: 2014 IEEE Wireless Commun. Networking Conference (WCNC 2014), pp. 469–474 (2014)
10. Molisch, A.F.: Wireless Communications, 2nd edn. Wiley (2010)
11. Essiambre, R., Kramer, G., Winzer, P.J., Foschini, G.J., Goebel, B.: Capacity limits of optical fiber networks. Journal of Lightwave Technology 28(4), 662–701 (2010)
12. Winzer, P.J.: Modulation and multiplexing in optical communication systems. IEEE LEOS Newsletter 23, 4–10 (2007)
13. Cartledge, J., Krause, D., Roberts, K., Laperle, C., McGhan, D., Sun, H., Wu, K.-T., Sullivan, M.O., Jiang, Y.: Electronic signal processing for fiber-optic communications. IEEE LEOS Newsletter 23, 11–15 (2007)
14. Weiss, L.G.: Wavelets and wideband correlation processing. IEEE Signal Process. Mag. 11(1), 13–32 (1994)
15. Spangenberg, S.M., Schott, I., McLaughlin, S., Povey, G.J., Cruickshank, D.G., Grant, P.M.: An FFT-based approach for fast acquisition in spread spectrum communication systems. Wireless Personal Communications 13, 27–56 (2000)
16. Herman, M.A., Strohmer, T.: High-resolution radar via compressed sensing. IEEE Trans. Signal Process. 57(6), 2275–2284 (2009)
17. Bajwa, W.U., Gedalyahu, K., Eldar, Y.C.: Identification of parametric underspread linear systems and super-resolution radar. IEEE Trans. Signal Process. 59(6), 2548–2561 (2011)

Appendix

A   A Complementary Pair of TD and FD Correlators

The outputs of a complementary pair of FD and TD integrators are defined by

$$c_{\boldsymbol{p},n'}^{\mathrm{GD(TD)}}[\mu;\hat{\ell}_d] = \sum_\ell r[\ell]\overline{u}_{n'}^{\mathrm{TD}}[\ell - pNM - \hat{\ell}_d; \mathcal{Y}]$$

$$\times W_L^{((\mu+p'N'M'+n'M')(\ell-\frac{pNM+\hat{\ell}_d}{2})+\overline{\varphi}_{\mathrm{comp}}^{\mathrm{GD(TD)}}(\hat{\ell}_d,\mu))},$$

$$(n' = 1, 2, \ldots, N'), \tag{24}$$

$$C_{\boldsymbol{p},n}^{\mathrm{GD(FD)}}[\sigma;\hat{k}_D] = \sum_k R[k]\overline{U}_n^{\mathrm{FD}}[k - p'N'M' - \hat{k}_D; \mathcal{Y}]$$

$$\times W_L^{-((\sigma+pNM+nM)(k-\frac{p'N'M'+\hat{k}_D}{2})+\overline{\varphi}_{\mathrm{comp}}^{\mathrm{GD(FD)}}(\sigma,\hat{k}_D))},$$

$$(n = 1, 2, \ldots, N), \tag{25}$$

where $u_{n'}^{\mathrm{TD}}[\ell; \mathcal{Y}]$ and $U_n^{\mathrm{FD}}[k; \mathcal{Y}]$ are TD and FD template waveforms, defined by

$$u_{n'}^{\mathrm{TD}}[\ell; \mathcal{Y}] = \frac{1}{\sqrt{N}} \sum_{n=0}^{N-1} Y_{nn'} W_L^{-nn'MM'/2} z[\ell - nM], \tag{26}$$

$$U_n^{\mathrm{FD}}[k; \mathcal{Y}] = \frac{1}{\sqrt{N'}} \sum_{n'=0}^{N'-1} Y'_{n'} W_L^{nn'MM'/2} Z[k - n'M']. \tag{27}$$

Eqs.(24) and (25) for $\boldsymbol{q} = \boldsymbol{p}$ and $\mathcal{Y} = \mathcal{X}$ are evaluated as

$$\Re\left\{c_{\boldsymbol{p},n'}^{\mathrm{GD(TD)}}[\mu;\hat{\ell}_d]\right\} = \frac{\alpha}{\sqrt{N'}}\tilde{\theta}_{zz}[\hat{\ell}_d - \ell_d, \mu - k_D] \cdot \mathrm{sinc}(NM(\mu - k_D)/L)$$

$$\cdot \cos(\frac{2\pi}{L}\{\beta_0 + \bar{\delta}(\hat{\ell}_d,\mu) + n'M'(\hat{\ell}_d - \ell_d) - \frac{N+1}{2}M(\mu - k_D)), \tag{28}$$

$$\Re\left\{C_{\boldsymbol{p},n}^{\mathrm{GD(FD)}}[\sigma;\hat{k}_D]\right\} = \frac{\alpha}{\sqrt{N}}\tilde{\theta}_{ZZ}[\hat{k}_D - k_D, -(\sigma - \ell_d)] \cdot \mathrm{sinc}(N'M'(\sigma - \ell_d)/L)$$

$$\cdot \cos(\frac{2\pi}{L}\{\beta_0 + \bar{\Delta}(\sigma,\hat{k}_D) + \frac{N'+1}{2}M'(\sigma - \ell_d) - nM(\hat{k}_D - k_D)). \tag{29}$$

Note that the sinc functions in Eqs.(28) and (29) suggest that $|\mu - k_D| < 1/(NM)$ and $|\sigma - \ell_d| < 1/(N'M')$ are necessary for such integrator outputs to have peak values. Namely, controlled parameters μ and σ must be very close to k_D and ℓ_d. On the contrary, the ambiguity functions in Eqs.(28) and (29) imply that $|\hat{\ell}_d - \ell_d| < 3\sigma_t$ and $|\hat{k}_D - k_D| < 3\sigma_f$ are necessary for the prescribed values. Hence, high accuracy is not required for $\hat{\ell}_d$ and $\hat{k}_D$.

B   Definitions of Several Phase Terms

The phase terms $\bar{\delta}(\hat{\ell}_d, \mu)$ and $\bar{\Delta}(\sigma, \hat{k}_D)$, mentioned in (9) and (10), are defined as

$$\bar{\delta}(\hat{\ell}_d, \mu) = (pq' - p'q)NMN'M'$$
$$- \begin{vmatrix} (p+q)NM & (p'+q')N'M' \\ \hat{\ell}_d - \ell_d & \mu - k_D \end{vmatrix} + \begin{vmatrix} \hat{\ell}_d & \mu \\ \ell_d & k_D \end{vmatrix}, \tag{30}$$

$$\bar{\Delta}(\sigma, \hat{k}_D) = (pq' - p'q)NMN'M'$$
$$- \begin{vmatrix} (p+q)NM & (p'+q')N'M' \\ \sigma - t_d & \hat{k}_D - k_D \end{vmatrix} + \begin{vmatrix} \sigma & \hat{k}_D \\ \ell_d & k_D \end{vmatrix}. \tag{31}$$

The phase terms $\bar{\varphi}_{\text{orig}}^{\text{GD(TD)}}$, $\bar{\varphi}_{\text{orig}}^{\text{GD(FD)}}$, $\bar{\varphi}_{\text{comp}}^{\text{GD(TD)}}$, and $\bar{\varphi}_{\text{comp}}^{\text{GD(FD)}}$ are defined as

$$\bar{\varphi}_{\text{orig}}^{\text{GD(FD)}}(\hat{\ell}_d, \mu) = \frac{1}{2}\begin{vmatrix} pNM & p'N'M' \\ \hat{\ell}_d & \mu \end{vmatrix} + \frac{1}{2}\begin{vmatrix} nM & 0 \\ \hat{\ell}_D + pNM & \mu + p'N'M' \end{vmatrix}, \tag{32}$$

$$\bar{\varphi}_{\text{orig}}^{\text{GD(TD)}}(\sigma, \hat{k}_D) = \frac{1}{2}\begin{vmatrix} pNM & p'N'M' \\ \sigma & \hat{k}_D \end{vmatrix} + \frac{1}{2}\begin{vmatrix} 0 & n'M' \\ \sigma + pNM & \hat{k}_D + p'M' \end{vmatrix}, \tag{33}$$

$$\bar{\varphi}_{\text{comp}}^{\text{GD(FD)}}(\sigma, \hat{k}_D) = \frac{1}{2}\begin{vmatrix} pNM & p'N'M' \\ \sigma & \hat{k}_D \end{vmatrix} + \frac{1}{2}\begin{vmatrix} nM & 0 \\ \sigma + pNM & \hat{k}_D + p'N'M' \end{vmatrix}, \tag{34}$$

$$\bar{\varphi}_{\text{comp}}^{\text{GD(TD)}}(\hat{\ell}_d, \mu) = \frac{1}{2}\begin{vmatrix} pNM & p'N'M' \\ \hat{\ell}_d & \mu \end{vmatrix} + \frac{1}{2}\begin{vmatrix} 0 & n'M' \\ \hat{\ell}_d + pNM & \mu + p'N'M' \end{vmatrix}. \tag{35}$$

Replacing μ and $\hat{\ell}_d$ in (32) with $\mu - \widetilde{k}_D$ and $\hat{\ell}_d - \widetilde{\ell}_d$ gives $\bar{\varphi}_{\text{orig,Act}}^{\text{GD(FD)}}$. Similarly, replacing σ and $\hat{k}_D$ in (33) with $\sigma - \widetilde{\ell}_d$ and $\hat{k}_D - \widetilde{k}_D$ gives $\bar{\varphi}_{\text{orig,Act}}^{\text{GD(TD)}}$.

Filter Design for Identification
in Multiple Access Channel

Sergey Bogoslovsky[1] and Andrey Trofimov[2]

[1] JSC "Radar mms", Saint-Petersburg, Russia
bogoslovsky_sv@radar-mms.com
[2] Saint-Petersburg State University of Aerospace Instrumentation,
Saint-Petersburg, Russia
andrei.trofimov@vu.spb.ru

Abstract. Identification problem in a multiple access channel is being studied. Such problem arises, for example, in analysis of monitoring systems using the surface acoustic wave (SAW) radio tag (label). The SAW radio tags are the passive wireless units which can be used in different application with extreme environment factors (high temperature, radiation, *etc*). The mathematical model of radio tag is assumed to be a linear time-invariant filter. A receiver (reader) observes the sum of the K linear filters responses to an interrogation signal. A combination of K filters are chosen arbitrary from the known set of M known filters, $K << M$. Receiver determines the filter combination according to the sum response received. The problem of the design of the radio label impulse responses under some constraints is studied.

Keywords: Multiple access, surface acoustic wave, pulse response, linear chirp signal, forming filter, information filter, combined filter, error-correcting code, cross-correlation.

1 Introduction and Problem Formulation

1.1 Basic Model

There exists a set of M linear time-invariant filters with known pulse responses of the finite duration $h_m(t)$, $m = 0,1,...,M-1$. A subset of K filters with different pulse responses $h_{m_1}(t), h_{m_2}(t),..., h_{m_K}(t)$, $m_k \in \{0,1,...,M\}$, $k = 1,2,...,K$, belonging to the set $\{h_m(t)\}$ is in scope. Interrogation signal $x(t)$ enters the K filters simultaneously and the sum of the filter responses coming with random delays and corrupted by an additive noise is observed at the receiver side. The general system model is shown in Fig. 1.

The model shown in Fig.1 can describe several real situations. For example, it can describe a transmission over K parallel channels with a filter and additive noise. In this case the receiver analyzes the channel output signal $r(t)$ and determines

M. Jonsson et al. (Eds.): MACOM 2014, LNCS 8715, pp. 16–28, 2014.
© Springer International Publishing Switzerland 2014

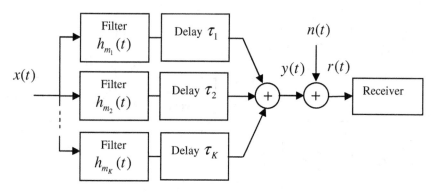

Fig. 1. System model

transmitted signal $x(t)$. The scheme of the radio frequency identification (RFID) with collisions [1,2,3] can be another variant described by the model depicted in Fig.1. In this case the receiver estimates the filter indexes $m_1, m_2, ..., m_K$ by the received signal $r(t)$. In such formulation the filter impulse responses $\{h_m(t)\}$, $m_k \in \{0,1,...,M\}$, and the input signal $x(t)$ should be designed in such a way that would be possible to estimate the filter indexes $m_1, m_2, ..., m_K$ with sufficient reliability. Problem in this formulation is examined in this paper.

One of the ways of the physical implementation of such filters is based on the principles of functional electronics. Currently the most used devices are the units using surface acoustic wave (SAW). The SAW based technologies can create a number of electronic devices: band-pass filters, delay lines, resonator. The distinctive feature of these devices is their frequency range from 1MHz to 5MHz corresponding to the modern requirements to radio frequency identification (RFID) systems. The practical applications could be, for example, monitoring systems, access control to a given zone *etc*. The usage of SAW radio label allows to create devices working in extreme environment: at temperature from -196°C to +1000°C and high radiation, where semiconductor-based units cannot operate. The existing techniques of the SAW filter design can implement the devices with various complicated impulse responses: linear chirp, BPSK, QPSK, *etc*. The SAW devices in most cases can be described as linear time-invariant filter and we hereafter use this model.

Note that a dual interpretation is possible for this problem formulation. In this interpretation one can consider transmission of the "signals" $h_{m_1}(t)$, $h_{m_2}(t)$,..., $h_{m_K}(t)$ over the multiple access channel with the filter $x(t)$. The equivalent diagram is shown in Fig.2.

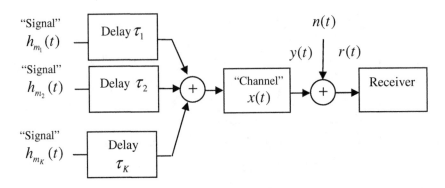

Fig. 2. Dual equivalent system model

1.2   Formal Description

Let $x(t)$ be an input signal of the set of K filters. Then the signal at the receiver input is given as

$$r(t) = y(t) + n(t) = \sum_{k=1}^{K} y_{m_k}(t - \tau_k) + n(t),$$

where $y(t) = \sum_{k=1}^{K} y_{m_k}(t - \tau_k)$ is the total response of the filter set, τ_k is the delay of the response of the k th filter, $y_m(t) = x(t) * h_m(t)$ is the m th filter response, $*$ denotes convolution operation, $n(t)$ is the white Gaussian process with zero mean and two-sided spectral power density $N_0/2$. The processing at the receiver side consists in identifying the filter set, i.e. in determining the index values $m_1, m_2, ..., m_K$ according to the received signal $r(t)$.

The problem of design of the identification system includes the task of the simultaneous design of the filter set with impulse responses $h_m(t)$, $m = 0, 1, ..., M - 1$, and the choice of the input interrogation signal $x(t)$. These functions must be designed in such a way that it is possible to identify any set of K filters with sufficient reliability. This problem can be divided into two: at first under given limitations choose the responses $y_m(t)$, $m = 0, 1, ..., M - 1$, and secondly under given limitations constructing the filters $h_m(t)$, $m = 0, 1, ..., M - 1$, and input interrogation signal $x(t)$ giving the required responses.

The trivial solution could be the following. Let us choose responses $y_m(t)$, $m = 0, 1, ..., M - 1$, so that they are sufficiently distinguishable by, for example, correlation receiver. Such functions can be constructed using the discrete sequences with good cross-correlations (see *e.g.* [5]). If we now assume that the filter impulse responses are $h_m(t) = y_m(t)$ and input signal is assigned as $x(t) = \delta(t)$, then the problem can be considered resolved. In practice the δ-function can be approximated by sufficiently short pulse signal. However in many cases such approach is unacceptable due to the limitations imposed on the shape of the input signal $x(t)$. Usually there exist limitations on the bandwidth and duration of the input signal $x(t)$ and the response signals $y_m(t)$, and also on duration of the filter impulse responses $h_m(t)$, $m = 0,1,...,M-1$.

In the next Section we present an approach to solving this problem. Our solution uses a special design of the filter (radio tag) consisting of concatenation of the forming and information filters. An example is presented in Section 3, and the concluding remarks are given in Section 4.

2   Possible Solution

2.1   Constraints

In this study we assume that constraints consist of the following: a) duration of each filter impulse response $h_m(t)$, $m = 0,1,...,M-1$, does not exceed given value, b) frequency spectrum of the input signal $x(t)$ and the spectrum of each response signal $y_m(t)$, $m = 0,1,...,M-1$, are localized around a central frequency f_c, c) bandwidth of the input signal and response signals does not exceed the value W, $W \ll f_c$, and d) duration of the input signal does not exceed the value T_x. We assume here some obvious, or "practical", definition of the signal bandwidth and duration to avoid the possible rigorous contradiction between conditions "c" and "d". In addition, to transmit maximum energy under constraints imposed on the impulse power prescribed by the administrative regulations it is necessary to keep the constant amplitude of the interrogation signal at maximum possible level. It means that interrogation signal must be chosen as a more or less wideband waveform with constant amplitude; for instance, linear chirp signal.

2.2   Impulse Responses

Let us consider impulse responses of *some* filters $c_m(t)$, $m = 0,1,...,M-1$, constructed as sequences of the elementary signals (chips), where the specific combination of the chips is defined by a discrete sequence chosen from a set of the sequences with given correlations. An example could be FSK and code words of a correcting code.   We further assume that impulse responses of the filters are constructed using the FSK signals with $\text{sinc}(\cdot)$ [1] envelope, i.e. they are sequences of chips

$$\varphi_i(t;T_c) = \sqrt{2/T_c}\,\text{sinc}(t/T_c)\cos(2\pi f_i t), \tag{1}$$

where $\text{sinc}(x) = \sin \pi x/(\pi x)$, f_i is the i th frequency, $f_i > 1/2T_c$, $i = 0,1,...,q-1$, q is number of frequencies, $q \geq 2$. The frequencies f_i are chosen so that $f_i = f_0 + i\Delta_f$, where $\Delta_f = 1/T_c$, $i = 0,1,...,q-1$. For this choice of the frequencies the functions $\varphi_i(\cdot;T_c)$ и $\varphi_k(\cdot;T_c)$ are orthogonal for $i \neq k$. The coefficient $\sqrt{2/T_c}$ in the right-hand part of the equation (1) provides the condition $\|\varphi_i(t;T_c)\| = 1$, where $\|\cdot\|$ is denotation for Euclidean norm. The spectrum of the function $\varphi_i(t;T_c)$, $i = 0,1,...,q-1$, is localized around the frequency f_i and its bandwidth is $1/T_c$. The total band is limited by the values $f_{\min} = f_0 - (2T_c)^{-1}$ and $f_{\max} = f_{q-1} + (2T_c)^{-1} = f_0 + (2q-1)/(2T_c)$, and the total bandwidth is equal to $W = q/T_c$. We assume hereafter that signal parameters are chosen so that frequency spectrum occupies the whole assigned frequency band.

The functions $\varphi_i(t;T_c)$, as it follows from (1), are defined on the whole time axis. In practice it is sufficient to consider the segments of these functions defined on interval $[-N_p T_c, N_p T_c]$, where $N_p = 3...10$.

Impulse response for each filter is built as a *sequence* of *overlapped* elementary signal defined by the equation (1). The specific signal sequence is defined by an index sequence (or multi-index) $\mathbf{i} = (i_0, i_1, ..., i_{N-1})$ as follows

$$c_m(t) = \sum_{l=0}^{N-1} \varphi_{i_l}(t - lT_c; T_c). \tag{2}$$

Evidently, the filter index m and multi-index $\mathbf{i}$ are in one-to-one correspondence.

Some properties of the functions $\varphi_i(t;T_c)$ defined by (1) are useful in the further consideration.

Property 1

$$\varphi_i(t;T_c) * \varphi_k(t;T_c) = \begin{cases} \sqrt{T_c/2}\,\varphi_i(t;T_c) = \text{sinc}(t/T_c)\cos(2\pi f_i t), & i = k, \\ 0, & i \neq k. \end{cases} \tag{3}$$

---

[1] The study of the elementary signal with constant envelope is possible as well, but it requires taking into account more technical details.

Property 2.   Let $\rho_{ik}(t)$ be cross-correlation of the functions $\varphi_i(t;T_c)$ and $\varphi_k(t;T_c)$, $\rho_{ik}(t) = \int_{-\infty}^{\infty} \varphi_i(x;T_c)\varphi_k(x-t;T_c)dx$. Since $\varphi_i(t;T_c)$ and $\varphi_k(t;T_c)$ are even functions then

$$\rho_{ik}(t) = \varphi_i(t;T_c) * \varphi_k(t;T_c). \tag{4}$$

Property 3. Let function $u_0(t)$ be defined as

$$u_0(t) = \varphi_{i_c}(t;1/W) = \sqrt{2W}\operatorname{sinc}(Wt)\cos(2\pi f_{i_c}t), \tag{5}$$

where $W = q/T_c$, $f_{i_c} = (f_0 + f_{q-1})/2$. It means that the spectrum of the function $u_0(t)$ is localized in the center of the frequency interval $[f_{min}, f_{max}]$ and its width is W. Then

$$\varphi_i(t;T_c) * u_0(t) = \frac{1}{\sqrt{2W}}\varphi_i(t;T_c) = \frac{1}{\sqrt{WT_c}}\operatorname{sinc}(t/T_c)\cos(2\pi f_i t). \tag{6}$$

Corollary. It follows from the equations (6) and (2) that if the filter impulse responses are chosen as $h_m(t) = c_m(t)$, where $c_m(t)$ are defined by the equation (2), and the input signal is assigned as $x(t) \propto u_0(t)$ (the sign $\propto$ hereafter denotes proportionality), then for the response of the m th filter, $m = 0,1,...,M-1$, the following equation is valid

$$y_m(t) = x(t) * h_m(t) \propto u_0(t) * c_m(t) \propto c_m(t). \tag{7}$$

Suppose that the pulse responses $c_m(t)$ are *constructed* in such a way that their cross-correlations provide an acceptable distinction in identification process. Then if the input signal is assigned as $x(t) = K_x u_0(t)$, where K_x is a positive coefficient, then the problem can be considered as solved, because, as it follows from the equation (7), the correlations of the responses $y_m(t)$ coincide with the correlations of the functions $c_m(t)$. However the input signal $x(t) = K_x u_0(t)$ may be *unacceptable* if the constraints on the shape of the input interrogation signal exist. In the next subsection we show how to solve this problem.

2.3   Forming and Information Filters

Let us consider a hypothetical structure representing concatenation of the filters as it is shown in Fig.3. The first filter with pulse response $g(t)$ is designed to form the

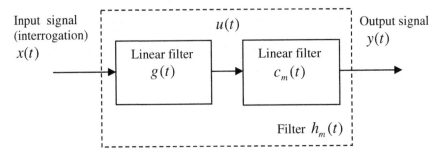

Fig. 3. Concatenation of the filters

signal $u(t)$ which would provide an *acceptable* response $y(t)$ at the second filter output. Further we call the first filter shown in Fig.3 as a *forming* filter, the second filter as an *information* one, and their concatenation as a *combined* filter.

We assume as before that pulse responses of the information filters are chosen so that their cross-correlations provide an acceptable distinction of the output signals.

The task can be reduced to a) choice of the shape of the interrogation signal $x(t)$, satisfying given constraints, and b) construction of the *forming filter* $g(t)$ providing the signal $u(t)$ close enough to the optimal signal $u_0(t)$ given by the equation (4).

Suppose that the function $x(t)$ and $g(t)$ are found in such a way that $u(t) \propto u_0(t)$, i.e. $x(t) * g(t) \propto u_0(t)$. Then one can write that

$$y_m(t) = x(t) * h_m(t) = x(t) * g(t) * c_m(t) \propto u_0(t) * c_m(t) \propto c_m(t).$$

The condition $x(t) * g(t) \propto u_0(t)$ cannot be satisfied *exactly* under the constraints imposed on the shape of function $x(t)$ и $g(t)$. We show how this condition can be fulfilled approximately.

2.4   Linear Chirp Signal and Forming Filter

An acceptable choice of the functions $x(t)$ и $g(t)$ can be done as follows in the following. Let the signal $x(t)$ be a linear chirp signal

$$x(t) = \begin{cases} \sqrt{2/T_x} \cos 2\pi(f_c t + \beta t^2 / 2), & -T_x/2 < t < T_x/2, \\ 0, & \text{otherwise}, \end{cases} \tag{8}$$

where T_x is the signal duration, f_c is the central frequency, β is frequency sweep coefficient, $\beta = W / T_x$, W is bandwidth of the chirp signal[2], $W = \beta T_x$. Then if the forming filter is the matched filter to the signal $x(t)$, i.e. if

---

[2] We assume hereafter that band of input signal $x(t)$ and band of the responses are the same.

$$g(t) = K_g x(T_x - t),$$

(9)

where K_g is a properly chosen positive constant, then the filter output $u(t) = x(t) * g(t)$ is close to the function $u_0(t)$ when $\beta T_x \gg 1$. This can be explained as follows. The forming filter output signal can be represented as

$$u(t) = \int_{-\infty}^{\infty} x(\tau) g(t-\tau) d\tau = K_g \int_{-\infty}^{\infty} x(\tau) x(T_x - t + \tau) d\tau = K_g k_x(t - T_x),$$

(10)

where $k_x(\tau)$ is the correlation function of the signal $x(t)$, $k_x(\tau) = \int_{-\infty}^{\infty} x(t) x(t+t) d\tau$. It is known (see e.g. [6]) that the correlation function of the signal (8) is close to a function proportional to the function $u_0(t)$, defined by the formula (5). The expression for the correlation function of the chirp signal is rather complex and it can be written as

$$k_x(\tau) = \frac{A^2}{2} \left[\frac{1}{2\sqrt{\beta}} \left(\cos(c)(C(U_2) - C(U_1)) - \sin(c)(S(U_2) - S(U_1)) \right) + \right.$$

$$\left. + \left(T_2 + \frac{f_0}{\beta} + \frac{\tau}{2} \right) \text{sinc}(Y_2) - \left(T_1 + \frac{f_0}{\beta} + \frac{\tau}{2} \right) \text{sinc}(Y_1) \right],$$

(11)

where $C(x)$ and $S(x)$ are the Fresnel integrals, $C(x) = \int_0^x \cos(\pi u^2 / 2) du$ и $S(x) = \int_0^x \sin(\pi u^2 / 2) du$, $c = 2\pi \left(-\beta(\tau + 2f_0 / \beta)^2 / 4 + f_0 \tau + \beta \tau^2 / 2 \right)$, and

$$T_1 = \max(-T_x / 2, -T_x / 2 - \tau), \quad T_2 = \min(T_x / 2, T_x / 2 - \tau),$$
$$U_1 = (2T_1 + \tau + 2f_0 / \beta)\sqrt{\beta}, \quad U_2 = (2T_2 + \tau + 2f_0 / \beta)\sqrt{\beta},$$
$$Y_1 = 2(\beta T_1 \tau + f_0 \tau + \beta \tau^2 / 2), \quad Y_2 = 2(\beta T_2 \tau + f_0 \tau + \beta \tau^2 / 2).$$

Note that in the most interesting cases the first term in the brackets in the right hand part of (11) can be neglected [6].

To finalize the description the concatenated structure shown in Fig.3 we obtain the value of the coefficient K_g in (9) ensuring the equality $\|u\|^2 = \|x\|^2$. Assume to a first approximation that the amplitude spectrum $|X(f)|$ is constant in the band $|f \pm f_c| < W / 2$. Then using equation (10) one can show that $K_g = \sqrt{2W}$.

Now we can describe the constructed set of the *combined* filters $\{h_m(t)\}$, $m = 0,1,...,M-1$, and input interrogation signal $x(t)$, suggested for the solving the identification problem. It is assumed that the set of the information filters impulse responses $c_m(t)$, $m = 0,1,...,M-1$, given by the equation (2) are constructed. These filters can be designed, for example, with the usage of the discrete sequences with good cross-correlations, but the problem of that design is *not in the scope* of this paper. Impulse responses of the combined filters used for identification are built as $h_m(t) = g(t)*c_m(t)$, where $g(t)$ is the filter matched to the interrogation signal $x(t)$ given by (8).

3   Example

Consider an abstract illustrative example. Suppose that the number of frequencies $q = 11$ and the frequency values are assigned so that $f_i = f_0 + i/T_c$, $i = 0,1,...,10$, and $f_0 T_c = 35$. The total bandwidth $W = q/T_c = 11/T_c$. Assume that the chip duration in (1) is limited as $6T_c$, i.e. the chip is defined on the time interval $[-3T_c, 3T_c]$.

3.1   Input Signal and Forming Filter

Let the input signal be given by the equation (8) and its duration $T_x = 15T_c$. Duration of the forming filter pulse response $g(t)$ is also equal to T_x. It is important to provide closeness of the function $u(t)$ и $u_0(t)$ defined by formulas (10) and (5) respectively. The results of calculation of the function $k_x(\tau) \propto u(\tau)$ for $\tau \geq 0$ are shown in Fig. 4. The function $\mathrm{sinc}(Wt)\cos(2\pi f_c t) \propto u_0(\tau)$, is also shown in Fig.4; the function $u_0(t)$ is defined by the equation (5).

3.2   Information and Combined Filters

Let the impulse responses of the information filters consist of $N = 10$ *overlapped* elements (chips) of duration $6T_c$. Then the duration of the *information filter* pulse responses is equal $T_h = 15T_c$. We assume that this duration satisfies the constraints.

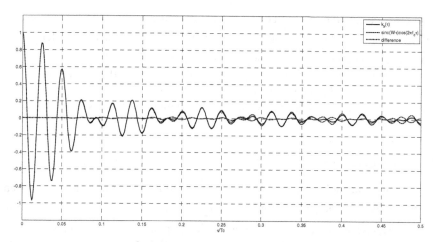

Fig. 4. Correlation function $k_x(\tau)$, function $\mathrm{sinc}(W_x\tau)\cos(2\pi f_0\tau)$ and their difference

Suppose for example that impulse responses are constructed using a subset of the coset of Reed-Solomon code $(10, 3)$ with the minimum distance of 8 over the finite field $GF(11)$. The code and each of its cosets contains $11^3 = 1331$ words and it is possible to select $M = 128$ words with acceptable relative level of cross-correlation ≤ 0.4. Note that the *construction* of the sequence with given values of cross correlation is *not in scope* of this study and this set of sequences is just *simple illustrative example*.

Example of an information filter impulse response and impulse response of the corresponding combined filter are shown in Fig.5

The Fig.6 shows the maximums of the normalized cross-correlations of the information filters impulse responses (left), and the maximums of the normalized cross-correlations of the combined filter responses on the linear chirp signal (right).

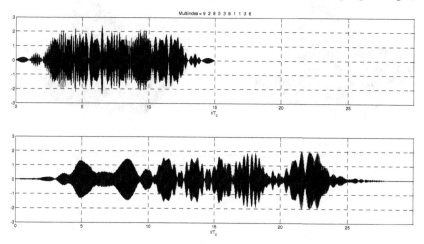

Fig. 5. Impulse responses of an information filter and corresponding combined filter

The cross-correlations presented in Fig.6 are computed at the time lags not greater than $2T_c$. This condition corresponds to the maximum values of the delays τ_m (see.Fig.1) having a practical interest. It follows from the Fig.6 that in both cases the cross-correlations are very close. This means that the properties of the combined filter responses on the chirp signal are close to the properties of the desired responses constructed using the sequences belonging to the coset of the Reed-Solomon code.

3.3   Simulation Results

Plots of the simulated error probability as a function of signal-to-noise ratio are depicted in Fig. 7. The signal-to-noise ratio is defined as E/N_0, where E is the average response energy. Three options of the responses are considered: impulse response of the information filter (i.e. response of the information filter on δ-function), response of the information filter on the interrogation signal (5) defined on the time interval $[-3T_c, 3T_c]$, and the combined filter response on the linear chip signal. The curves for these three options are shown as the dashed, dotted and solid lines correspondingly. The simulation was performed for the number of simultaneous responses equal to $K = 2, 3, 4$ chosen with equal probabilities from $M = 128$ possible responses in each test.

As it follows from the Fig.6 the error probability for the suggested scheme is slightly more than error probability for the schemes with the interrogation signal of large (or even infinitely large) peak power.

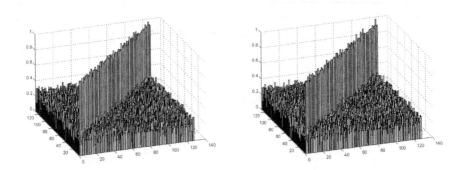

Fig. 6. Maximums of the normalized cross-correlations of the information filters impulse responses (left), and the maximums of the normalized cross-correlations of the combined filter responses on the linear chirp signal (right)

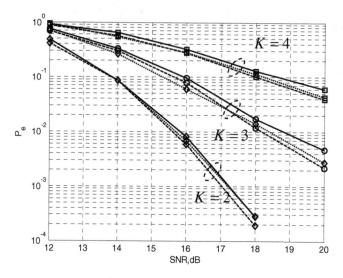

Fig. 7. Simulated identification error probability

3.4   Concluding Remarks

The proposed set of the filters for identification in the multiple access channel is constructed as concatenation of the *forming* and *information* filters. Each information filter has an *individual* pulse response and the forming filter has the *common* impulse response for all filters. Such design of the filters is the main result of this work. This structure allows to use the input signal with good energy properties and to provide response signals well distinguishable at the receiver side. Due to the usage of the forming filter the duration of the combined filter pulse response increases. This increase is acceptable in many cases. A separate task may be the study of the forming filter having the duration of its pulse response less than the duration of the input linear chirp signal but having the same bandwidth. This may reduce the duration of the combined filter impulse response when it is necessary.

Applying this approach allows to create highly energy effective SAW radio tag of the large information capacity for usage in the monitoring systems based on passive wireless devices.

References

1. Hartmann, C.S.: A global SAW ID tag with large data capacity. In: Proceedings of IEEE Ultrasonics Symposium, Münich, Germany, pp. 65–69 (2002)
2. Gallagher, D., Malocha, D., Puccio, D., Saldanha, N.: Orthogonal frequency coded filters for use in ultra-wideband communication systems. IEEE Trans. Ultrason. Ferroelectr. Freq. Control 55, 696–703 (2008)
3. Kozlovski, N.Y., Malocha, D.C., Weeks, A.R.: A 915 MHz SAW sensor correlate system. IEEE Sensors Journal 11(12) (December 2011)

4. Plessky, V.P., Reindl, L.M.: Review on SAW RFID Tags. In: Proceedings of IEEE Ultrasonics Symposium, vol. 57, pp. 654–668 (2010)
5. Pless, V.S., Huffman, W.C.: Handbook of Coding Theory. Elsevier Science B.V., Amsterdam (1998)
6. Cook, C.E., Bernfeld, M.: Radar signals. An introduction to theory and application, 568 p. Academic Press, NY (1967)

Reduced-Complexity Robust Detector in a DHA FH OFDMA System under Mixed Interference*

Dmitry Osipov[1,2]

[1] Institute for Information Transmission Problems
Russian Academy of Sciences,
19 Bolshoy Karetny Lane Moscow 127994, Russia
[2] National Research University Higher School of Economics,
20 Myasnitskaya Ulitsa Moscow 101000, Russia

Abstract. Future generation communication systems will have to endure interference induced by communication systems operating within the same frequency bands. Recently several coded DHA FH OFDMA systems employing rank-based detectors able to solve this problem were proposed. Unfortunately such detectors have relatively high complexity. In what follows a reduced-complexity detector using only column sorting for a coded DHA FH OFDMA employing a nonbinary convolutional inner code is proposed. The proposed detector is compared with the rank convolutional detector in terms of performance, complexity and delay.

Keywords: multiple access, coded DHA FH OFDMA, robust detector, reduced complexity.

1 Introduction

In the years to come interference will be the main factor limiting the performance of the wireless communication systems. This is due to the fact that the number of the frequency bands that can be used by the systems in question is limited, whereas the demand for wireless communication increases drastically.Therefore robust transmission and reception techniques are needed to provide reliable communications in the environment described above. One possible solution is a coded DHA FH OFDMA [1]: a coded OFDMA employing FSK in dynamically allocated frequency subbands. In [2] a robust detector for such a system employing inner block codes and order statistics-based metric has been proposed. Unfortunately the decoding algorithm employed in [2] boils down to exhaustive search thus precluding high rate codes usage due to complexity restrictions. For this reason in [3] it has been proposed to use inner convolutional codes in favor of the block ones. Convolutional codes can be decoded with the Viterbi decoder therefore higher rate codes can be used at the price of moderate complexity increase. However the complexity of the detector proposed in [3] is relatively high. In what follows a detector having lower complexity and better suited for hardware implementation is proposed.

---

* This work has been supported by the RFBR (research project No. 14-07-31197 mol_a).

M. Jonsson et al. (Eds.): MACOM 2014, LNCS 8715, pp. 29–34, 2014.

This paper is organized as follows. In section 2 a short sketch of a coded DHA FH OFDMA system is given. In section 3 a description of a rank decoder for q-ary convolutional code in a coded DHA FH OFDMA will be given and a reduced complexity decoder will be proposed. In section 4 the performance of the proposed detector will be investigated and the detector in question will be compared with the rank one in terms of performance, complexity and delay. Finally in section 5 the obtained results will be summarized .

2   A DHA FH OFDMA System: Transmission and Reception

Let us consider a multiple access system in which U_A active users transmit information via a channel split into Q identical nonoverlapping subchannels by means of OFDM. Information that is to be transmitted is encoded into a codeword of a terminated rate $R = b/c$ q-ary convolutional code ($q < Q$) from [3]. Whenever a user is to transmit a $q-$ary symbol it places 1 in the position of the vector $\bar{a}_g$ corresponding to the symbol in question within the scope of the mapping in use (in what follows it will be assumed that all the positions of the vector are enumerated from 1 to Q, moreover without loss of generality we shall assume that the 1st subchannel corresponds to 0, the 2nd subchannel corresponds to 1 and so on). Then a random permutation of the aforesaid vector is performed and the resulting vector $\pi_g(\bar{a}_g)$is used to form an OFDM symbol (permutations are selected equiprobably from the set of all possible permutations and the choice is performed whenever a symbol is to be transmitted). Therefore in order to transmit a codeword a user is to transmit n OFDM symbols. A sequence of OFDM symbols corresponding to a certain codeword that has been sent by a certain user will be referred to as a frame. Note that frames transmitted by different users need not be block synchronized, i.e. if within the time interval a certain user transmits a frame that corresponds to a codeword, symbols transmitted by another user within the same time period do not necessarily all comprise one codeword. Moreover, it will be assumed that transmissions from different users are uncoordinated, i.e. none of the users has information about the others. In what follows we shall assume that all users transmit information in OFDM frames and the transmission is quasisynchronous. In terms of the model under consideration this assumption means that transmissions from different users are symbol synchronized.

Within the scope of a certain codeword reception the receiver is to receive n OFDM symbols corresponding to the codeword in question. Note that the receiver is assumed to be synchronized with transmitters of all users. Therefore all the permutations done within the scope of transmission of the codeword in question are known to the user. The receiver measures energies at the outputs of all subchannels (let us designate the vector of the measurements as b_g where g is the number of the OFDM symbol) and applies inverse permutation to each vector b_g corresponding to the respective OFDM symbol thus reconstructing the initial order of elements and obtaining vector $\tilde{b}_g = \pi_g^{-1}(b_g)$. Let us consider a matrix X that consists of vectors $\tilde{b}_g = \pi_g^{-1}(b_g)$ that correspond to the codeword transmitted by the user under consideration. Let us consider the submatrix X_c (that is submatrix corresponding to the q first rows of the matrix X). Please note that X_c provides all the information necessary to decode the codeword.

3 Rank Detector and Reduced-Complexity Detector

Let us consider the detection problem. The straightforward detection algorithm boils down to computing the sums of the elements corresponding to the respective codewords and choosing the codeword corresponding to the maximum sum (maximum energy detector, MED). However severe interference can affect decision statistics that do not correspond to the transmitted codewords thus leading to erroneous decoding. Therefore a more robust metric is to be used. In [2] rank metric has been proposed. Let us first consider the indicator function

$$I(x^*, x) = \begin{cases} 1 \ x \leq x^* \\ 0 \ x > x^* \end{cases} \tag{1}$$

rank of the element of the matrix M_{ij} is given by

$$\rho(M_{ij}) = \sum_{k \neq i} \sum_{m \neq j} I(M_{ij}, M_{km}) \tag{2}$$

Please note that even if the value of a certain element increases drastically increase of the rank of the respective element is much smaller. Therefore rank detector is far more robust to interference than the conventional maximum energy detector. In [3] a detector based on the Viterbi algorithm has been proposed. The decoder computes rank sums for each branch of the trellis. At each node a path corresponding to the maximum rank sum is chosen. Thus the detector chooses the codeword corresponding to the path with maximum rank sum. In a sense the detector uses ranks of the respective matrix elements as reliability values.

One of the major drawbacks of the detector considered above (as well as its block counterpart proposed in [2]) is that it requires rank matrix calculation. The latter operation requires sorting of the elements of the $n \times q$ size matrix (where n is the inner codeword length). Moreover in the case under consideration the decoding delay is lower bounded by the frame duration. We are aiming at modifying the detector under consideration in order to decrease both the computational complexity and the decoding delay.

Please note that the rank decoder is based on the assumption that the fraction of elements having relatively high rank in the vector of matrix elements corresponding to the transmitted codeword is great. Therefore hereinafter we shall use the following approach: let us assume that each column of the matrix X_c is sorted in the descending order. Let us designate the $t - th$ element of the vector α_j obtained by sorting the $j - th$ column of the matrix X_c in the descending order by $\alpha_j(t)$. Let us consider the matrix D_t

$$D_t(i,j) = \begin{cases} 1 & X_c(i,j) \geq \alpha_j(t) \\ 0 & X_c(i,j) < \alpha_j(t) \end{cases} \tag{3}$$

Please note that each column of the matrix D_t contains exactly t nonzero entries. The nonzero entries in a certain column correspond to the elements of the respective column having values equal or greater than $t - th$ q quantile of this column. The matrix D_t is then used as an input for the Viterbi decoder i.e. the Viterbi decoder uses the matrix D_t to compute the respective branch metrics just the way it used rank matrix in the rank decoder. Please note that since the proposed detector utilizes only the information obtained by sorting the columns of the matrix X_c it is a suboptimal decoder and therefore it is bound to experience certain performance degradation. In what follows performance loss caused by the proposed detector (as compared to the rank one) will be investigated and the detector in question will be compared with the rank one in terms of performance, complexity and delay.

4   Simulation

An OFDM system with $N = 4096$ subcarriers has been considered (3276 being available to the users). A lognormal path loss model [4] has been considered with a typical distance of $d_0 = 100\,m$ and the radius of the cell $d_{\max} = 3\,km$ and 802.11 b model has been used to describe small-scale fading. A "pessimistic" simulation scenario has been used: within the scope of this scenario the user under consideration was assumed to be at the edge of the cell, whereas each of the interfering users was assumed to be at a distance of d (where d is equiprobably equal to $[d_0, 2d_0, 3d_0]$, distances being chosen at each instance.) Please note that no power control has been considered within the system under consideration i.e. the signals from the interfering users (at the receiver end) have powers much greater than of the signal from the user under consideration. The number of interfering users is equal to K. It has been assumed that the received signal is affected by the partial-band noise. The fraction of the effective bandwidth that is affected by the noise is given by $fr(0 < fr \leq 1)$ while the energy at the receiver end is described in terms of the signal to interference ratio SIR per bit. To provide sufficient rates and reasonable decoding complexity a rate $R = 2/10$ convolutional code obtained from (10,4,7) MDS convolutional code has been used.

In Fig. 1 and Fig. 2 dependencies of frame error rate (FER) on the value of the fraction of the bandwidth (occupied by the partial band noise) for different values of K(number of interfering narrowband signals) and L (number of information symbols) are presented. Please note that the overall codelength is given by $n = L \cdot c$) and SIR=-20 dB, c=10.

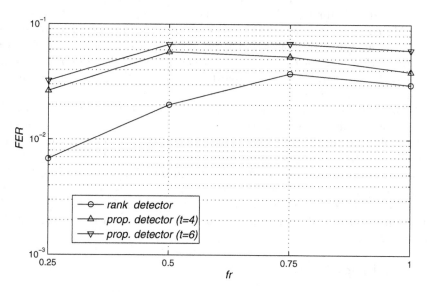

Fig. 1. Dependencies of the Frame Error Rate on the fraction fr for K=200,L=24

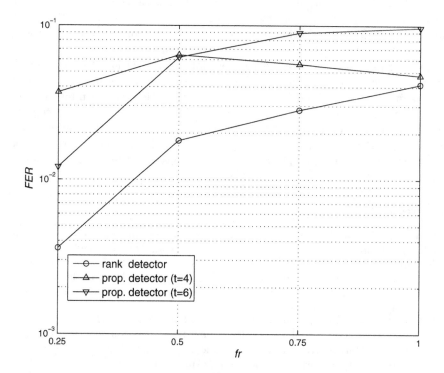

Fig. 2. Dependencies of the Frame Error Rate on the fraction fr for K=100,L=60

As can be seen form Fig. 1 and Fig. 2 for $t = 4$ the performance loss of the proposed detector (as compared to the rank one) is smaller than that for $t = 6$. Moreover the performance loss decreases as fr grows (in the case $t = 6$ the performance loss decreases much slower then in case of $t = 4$). In both cases the performance degradation is significant. Nevertheless in both cases the proposed detector provides acceptable frame error rates (even for $t = 6$ the probability of inner code erroneous decoding is less than 0.1). Thus employing Reed-Solomon codes as outer codes in a product-like construction can provide desirable probabilistic characteristics. The decision statistics computation for the proposed detector requires only sorting of the length q vector whereas the rank algorithm requires sorting of the length $N = qLc$. The rank detector proposed in [3] can start decoding only after the reception of a frame (i.e. Lc OFDM blocks). Since the proposed detector computes the necessary decision statistics for each OFDM block and is to compute branch metrics for each length c tuple of the inner code the decoding delay can be L times smaller than that of the rank decoder.

5   Conclusion

Hereinabove a reduced-complexity detector for a coded DHA FH OFDMA system with inner convolutional code is proposed. The detector in question uses column sorting for threshold computation in order to determine the list of candidate symbols for each position of the codeword. The resulting decision statistics matrix is then used as the the Viterbi decoder input.

Since the proposed detector replaces the global optimization that has been the key goal of the detector proposed in [3] with the suboptimal solution its application results in substantial performance degradation. However even under severe jamming the proposed detector provides probabilistic characteristics acceptable for real-life communication systems. At the same time both the complexity of the proposed detector and the required decoding delay are much smaller than that of the rank detector. Thus the detector considered hereinabove seems a promising candidate for real-life implementation.

References

1. Osipov, D., Frolov, A., Zyablov, V.: Multiple Access System for a Vector Disjunctive Channel. Problems of Information Transmission 48(3), 243–249 (2012)
2. Kondrashov, K., Afanassiev, V.: Ordered statistics decoding for semi-orthogonal linear block codes over random non-Gaussian channels. In: Proc. of the Thirteenth International Workshop on Algebraic and Combinatorial Coding Theory, Pomorie, Bulgaria, June 15-21, pp. 192–196 (2012)
3. Osipov, D.: Inner Convolutional Codes and Ordered Statistics Decoding in a Multiple Access System Enabling Wireless Coexistence. In: Jonsson, M., Vinel, A., Bellalta, B., Marina, N., Dimitrova, D., Fiems, D. (eds.) MACOM 2013. LNCS, vol. 8310, pp. 33–38. Springer, Heidelberg (2013)
4. Sklar, B.: Rayleigh fading channels in mobile digital communication systems. IEEE Communications Magazine 35(7), 90–100 (1997)

Measurements on V2V Communication Quality
in a Vehicle Platooning Application

Carl Bergenhem[1], Rolf Johansson[2], and Erik Coelingh[3]

[1] Qamcom Research and Technology, SE-412 18 Gothenburg, Sweden
carl.bergenhem@qamcom.se
(The experiments were done while employed at SP - Technical Research Institute of Sweden)
[2] SP - Technical Research Institute of Sweden, Dept. of Electronics, SE-501 15 Borås, Sweden
[3] Volvo Car Corporation, SE-405 31 Gothenburg, Sweden

Abstract. This paper presents results from measurements on Vehicle to Vehicle
(V2V) communication between participants in a cooperative application: vehicle platooning. The platoon being studied consists of four vehicles; one truck
in the lead and three passenger cars following. The V2V-communication node
in each vehicle contains an 802.11p radio tuned to 5.9 GHz. It is used to send
messages between vehicles to coordinate movements and maintain safety in the
platoon. In cooperative applications, V2V-communication is an enabling technology. The V2V-communication quality is studied according to packet error
rate. This is measured in tests with different speeds, antenna position and on
two tracks. The paper draws general conclusions on the performance of V2V-
communication and presents a comparison of the tested antenna placements on
the truck.

Keywords: Cooperative traffic application, vehicle to vehicle communication,
V2V, platooning.

1   Introduction

In this paper we present measurements on Vehicle to Vehicle (V2V) communication
for a cooperative application. In such an application, multiple entities cooperate to
solve a common goal such as platooning in road vehicles or formation flying in airborne vehicles. Each individual vehicle has local sensors but must also share data
from the sensors of other vehicles. This is because local sensors may be e.g. obscured
by other vehicles or have limited range. Additionally, commands for coordination,
such as joining or emergency brake, need to be exchanged. This is done with
V2V-communication which hence becomes an enabling technology for cooperative
systems. To design the cooperative function, the reliability and performance of the
V2V-communication must be known. The communication quality in different situations should be quantified to understand what must be handled by e.g. the control
algorithms of vehicle movements.

This paper presents results of tests on the V2V-communication system that
was implemented in the SARTRE-project. The tests were performed with multiple

M. Jonsson et al. (Eds.): MACOM 2014, LNCS 8715, pp. 35–48, 2014.

combinations of: Two different test tracks: a high speed oval circuit and a suburban general road track; Three different top speeds; Two different antenna placements on the truck: Dual antennas on the cabin roof and antennas on both rear view mirrors. In the tests each vehicle communicates and measures the packet error rate to each other vehicle. The paper draws general conclusions on the performance of V2V-communication and supports comparison of the tested antenna placements on the truck. We show how road curve geometry affects communication in this application. The results in this paper can be used e.g. to support the design of communication protocol for cooperative vehicle applications.

The rest of the paper is organized as follows: Related work is presented in the next section. Then follows a brief presentation of a cooperative application: SARTRE platooning. This is followed by a description of the measurement setup. The results of the tests are then presented and an analysis is made. Finally, conclusions are drawn.

2   Related Work

In [1] the focus is on channel measurements at street intersections for V2V-safety applications. Paper [2] presents range measurements for vehicles driving towards or away from each other. A survey of V2V-communication is done in [3]. It is shown that the channel characteristics vary depending on the type of road: (highway, rural, suburban and urban). This can be explained by the different velocities, surroundings (number of and distance to scatterers differs in open areas versus small cities), traffic intensity etc. All these variations affect the multipath propagation environment for the radio waves which in turn affects the channel quality.

In [4] it is experimentally shown to what degree that vehicles can obstruct the line of sight in a highway scenario. A channel model is presented and a relaying strategy is proposed that uses "tall vehicles" to gain an advantage in performance e.g. communication range. In [5] the periodic broadcasting on the control channel a 802.11p vehicular networks is modeled. The approach accounts for mutual influence among nodes, frequent periodic updates of broadcasted data, standard network advertisement procedures, and 802.11p prioritized channel access with multichannel-related phenomena. Various link quality conditions are investigated. This gives possible reasons for packet loss from the MAC layer perspective.

A measurement campaign that is similar to the one presented in this paper, is found in [6]. Here, tests involve two V2V-equiped vehicles and one antenna position. Consecutive packet loss, round trip delay of packets and communication range is investigated. These are other metric for the quality of the communication system. Other measurements of V2V-communication in a platooning application have been published [7]. These measurements are with five vehicles: two trucks and three cars and are focused on communication between the lead and following vehicles. In this paper measurements are focused on communication between all vehicles and show how road curve geometry affects communication in this application.

3   Cooperative Applications

Cooperative applications involve multiple entities that cooperate to solve a common goal. The entities can be vehicles and the goal can be a specific task such as platooning (road vehicles) or formation flying (airborne). The cooperative aspect of the application necessitates wireless communication among the participants of the application. In addition to vehicles, road-side units may also participate in the application e.g. to provide external information or high-level control. An example is traffic control that provides information on road condition and congestion. External data, i.e. not from a local sensor, is received from the source, e.g. other participants, at the local vehicle via V2V-communication.

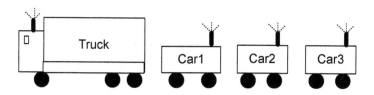

Fig. 1. The platoon

SARTRE (SAfe Road TRain for the Environment) was a European Commission Co-Funded FP7 project (2009 - 2012) that developed technology for platooning [8]. The project vision was to develop and integrate solutions that allow vehicles to drive in platoons. SARTRE defined a platoon (or road train) as a collection of vehicles led by a manually driven heavy lead vehicle. The following vehicles follow the lead vehicle automatically; both laterally and longitudinally. The demonstrator consisted of platooning with five vehicles: Two trucks and three passenger cars. Note that the measurements that are presented in this article focuses on four (one truck and three cars) of the five SARTRE vehicles. SARTRE aimed to explore technology for platooning on roads without changes to the infrastructure and that was safe enough to allow mixing with other users of public roads. Advantages of platooning included a reduction in fuel consumption, increased safety and increased driver convenience and comfort.

The technical challenges in the project were many and interesting, such as the design of control algorithm and sensor-fusion. Another challenge is the V2V-communication system. The V2V-node is a wireless gateway between the networks in the local vehicle to the networks in the other vehicles. The V2V-node allows sharing of local vehicle signals such as speed and sensor data among the vehicles in the platoon. The shared signals are used in the control algorithms of the platoon. The platoon forms a cooperative system where sensing, control algorithm and actuation are distributed throughout the platoon and data is communicated between vehicles. A brief survey of other vehicle platooning systems is given in [9]. Another example of cooperative application is formation flying of UAVs as studied in KARYON [10].

4   Measurement Setup

The SARTRE demonstrator for platooning (see Fig. 1) was used as a measurement platform with the difference that automatic control was not used. Instead, vehicles had manual longitudinal and lateral control except for cruise control in the lead vehicle. The target gap between vehicles is 13 m and was maintained based on driver judgment. The total length of the platoon (with four vehicles) was approx. 60 m. There were in total 12 different tested configurations with different combinations of three speeds, two antenna position and two tracks.

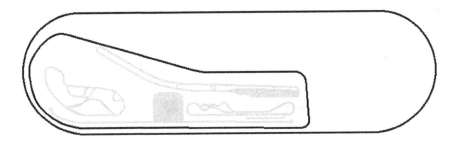

Fig. 2. The two test tracks

4.1   Track

The tests were done at the APPLUS IDIADA test grounds in Spain, see Fig. 2. The general road, 5.333 km long, is entirely within the large oval high speed circuit. On the high speed circuit, 7.493 km long, constant speed was possible with all platooning vehicles. The inner lane was used. Driving on both tracks is done clock-wise. On the general road the speed denotes the maximum speed for the test, i.e. the vehicles had to slow down (to 30 km/h lowest) in the curves. 50, 70 and 85 km/h targeted top speed was tested on both tracks. The environment at the track was: 16.5 C° and 1023 mbar air pressure. There was no rain and the tracks were dry. No other vehicles where on the track during the tests.

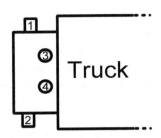

Fig. 3. The antenna placements on the truck as seen from above

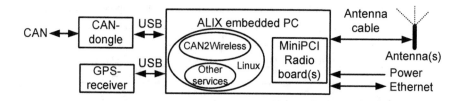

Fig. 4. The main components of the SARTRE V2V communication module

4.2   Antenna Placement

The order of the vehicles did not change during the tests, see Fig. 1. The truck is a "rigid", has double rear axles and carries a metal container. The antennas of the cars were placed on the centre of the roof; approx 1.5 m above the ground. The antenna configuration on the cars did not change during the tests. In the rest of the paper, when any antenna position is referred, such as roof, then this refers to the antenna position on the truck. Fig. 3 shows the two placements of antennas on the truck. At position 1 and 2 there are Mobile Mark RM3-5500 surface mount antennas with 5 dBi gain. These are mounted, with small metal brackets, on top of the side rear view mirrors. This position is denoted RVM in the paper. The height to the top of each mirror is 2.76 m. At position 3 and 4 there are Mobile Mark ECOM6-5500 stick antennas with 6 dBi gain. These are mounted with the magnet base on the cabin roof; each approximately 75 cm from the centre line of the cabin and 80 cm from the read edge of the cabin, i.e. edge of the container. The height of the cabin roof where the antenna is mounted is 3.8 m above the ground. The antenna is 26 cm high and thus barely reaches over the container at the rear (height 4 m).

4.3   Vehicle to Vehicle Communication Nodes

The V2V-nodes and software were developed at SP Technical Research Institute of Sweden and used in the SARTRE project. They are based on the x86 single board PC ALIX 3D3 and run Linux. The radios in the V2V-nodes use the Atheros AR5414 chipset. The V2V-nodes are connected to a GPS-receiver and can therefore log position etc. and synchronize the local clocks to UTC. The Ethernet connection is used for logging and maintenance. Fig. 4 shows an overview of the node. The radios use ITS-G5 [11], which is a set of protocols and parameters specified for a European profile of IEEE 802.11p, to transmit messages. The latter is an amendment to IEEE 802.11 [12] to add Wireless Access in Vehicular Environments (WAVE). 802.11p proposes modifications to the PHY and MAC layers (compared to IEEE 802.11a) in order to achieve a robust connection and a fast setup time for moving vehicles.

ITS-G5 operates in the frequency range (5855 - 5925 MHz) which is reserved for ITS applications (Intelligent Transport Systems) in Europe [11]. In this range there are three bands allocated: ITS-G5A (road safety), ITS-G5B (non-safety applications) and ITS-G5D (future applications). Similar spectrum bands have been allocated in the

Table 1. PER/SPER for roof antenna position on the high speed circuit

		Transmit					
	Average	Truck total	Truck left	Truck right	Car 1	Car 2	Car 3
Receive	Truck	-	-	-	3.12%	2.66%	2.34%
	Car 1	2.22%	5.24%	6.53%	-	0.26%	0.54%
	Car 2	1.91%	4.64%	4.66%	0.36%	-	0.52%
	Car 3	1.87%	4.31%	4.48%	0.51%	0.32%	-

		Transmit					
	Straight	Truck total	Truck left	Truck right	Car 1	Car 2	Car 3
Receive	Truck	-	-	-	3.16%	3.22%	3.24%
	Car 1	2.33%	5.32%	6.85%	-	0.24%	0.49%
	Car 2	2.18%	5.28%	5.93%	0.34%	-	0.47%
	Car 3	2.03%	5.16%	5.38%	0.45%	0.30%	-

	Right	Transmit					
	Curve	Truck total	Truck left	Truck right	Car 1	Car 2	Car 3
Receive	Truck	-	-	-	3.09%	2.10%	1.44%
	Car 1	2.11%	5.16%	6.21%	-	0.28%	0.59%
	Car 2	1.64%	4.01%	3.40%	0.39%	-	0.56%
	Car 3	1.70%	3.47%	3.57%	0.57%	0.34%	-

United States: 5850 - 5925 MHz, and in Japan: 5770 - 5850 MHz. The ETSI G5CC (Control Channel) is used in the tests in all vehicles. This is a channel allocation of the ITS-G5A band and has a centre frequency of 5900 MHz. The data rate that is used in the tests is 6 Mbit/s (the default rate). The output power from the node is configured to 20 dBm. This level complies with the EIRP power limit (33 dBm) of the channel that is used; provided that the antenna gain is less than 13 dBi. An overview of ITS communication and the various involved European standards such as ETSI ITS-G5 is given in [13]. Since the tests were carried out on a test track and that the ITS-band at the time of the tests was sparely populated, we assume that the tests are not affected by adjacent channel interference.

The packets that are broadcast from each V2V-node contain e.g. the GPS position of the sender, and have a data payload of 11 bytes. We note that a CAM message has a payload of approximately 300 -400 bytes depending on whether signature and security certificate is included [14]. The V2V-nodes broadcast packets every 25 ms at a fixed rate, i.e. 40 Hz. The number of sent packets is logged each second. Each node logs how many packets that it has sent and how many packets that are received from individual senders during one second. Collisions of packets and channel errors are not logged, i.e. these factors could not be directly noted in the results other than not receiving a packet at a node. We note that the update rate for CAM messages is between

1-10 Hz depending on the current dynamics of the vehicle, e.g. its velocity. The choice of a higher message update rate gives better resolution of results.

The V2V-node in the truck has two separate radios, each connected to one antenna and both tuned to the same channel (G5CC). The same packet is sent independently by both radios, i.e. two identical packets "in the air". The truck V2V-node hence sends twice as many packets as car V2V-nodes. The normal CSMA/CA multiple access protocol in 802.11 implies that the packets are not "in the air" simultaneously (i.e. causing a collision), but are interleaved. The drawback of the method is that it uses twice as much channel capacity (compared to the cars V2V-nodes) and is not compliant with ETSI. In the truck V2V-node incoming packets on each radio (antenna) are received separately. On reception of redundant packets only the first correctly received packets is accepted. This scheme with dual antennas was devised as a simple method to increase probability of correct reception of packets e.g. from the lead vehicle. Similar V2V-nodes are further described in [15].

5   Results

The results in this section show communication between all vehicles; the truck and cars. Measurements are done to assess quality of the V2V-system during steady-state platooning. Focus is on differences between the two antenna positions and the two tracks. The tests start with the vehicles in platoon-formation. Therefore maneuvering, such as acceleration/deceleration and lateral changes (turning) to form the platoon, is not included. Further we assume that the V2V-communication equipment does not suffer failure during the test. The measurements hence reflect the V2V-communication performance and differences of the antenna positions, tracks and speeds. All V2V-nodes transmit the same number of packets during the tests.

We measure Packet Error Rate (PER) and System Packet Error Rate (SPER) as the metric of quality of the V2V-system. They are statistical measures of the ratio of incorrectly received (e.g. corrupt) or transmitted but not received packets (e.g. lost) divided by the total number of sent packets. These two (e.g. incorrect or lost packets) are not differentiated between in the tests. PER concerns communication in a single channel. SPER concerns communication in a system which can contain redundant data channels between the communicating pair of nodes. For example, a truck sending to a car and a truck receiving from a car implies two channels in the system. The truck V2V-node sends each a packet over two antennas, i.e. two packets with identical information are sent from the vehicle; one from each radio. Any redundant (duplicate) packets that are received are disregarded. Car to car implies one channel in the system. In the tests there will hence be three different communication pairs, i.e. systems, see Fig. 5. The box signifies the communication system with the two pairs: sender to the left and receiver to the right. The circles imply radios/antennas. Due to limitations in the test logs, the PER of the two data channels in the a-configuration (car sending to truck) is not known; i.e. only SPER can be stated. A measurement of communication quality applies to a particular system, i.e. the configurations in the communicating pair of nodes. The SPER of the different systems cannot be directly compared, i.e. they are "apples and oranges", since the systems are not equivalent such as the a and b-configuration in Fig. 5. In a-configuration one packet is sent by the sending node and has two opportunities to be received at the receiver. In the b-configuration there are two packets sent and either can be received at the receiver. These two cases are not directly comparable.

Table 2. PER/SPER for RVM on the high speed circuit

Average	Transmit					
	Truck total	Truck left	Truck right	Car 1	Car 2	Car 3
Truck	-	-	-	2.26%	2.39%	2.79%
Car 1	1.61%	3.82%	4.69%	-	0.34%	0.64%
Car 2	2.32%	3.99%	4.19%	0.40%	-	0.58%
Car 3	2.42%	4.09%	4.48%	0.62%	0.34%	-

(Receive)

Straight	Transmit					
	Truck total	Truck left	Truck right	Car 1	Car 2	Car 3
Truck	-	-	-	1.70%	1.39%	1.38%
Car 1	1.78%	2.51%	5.98%	-	0.43%	0.62%
Car 2	1.66%	2.22%	4.22%	0.52%	-	0.60%
Car 3	1.51%	1.96%	4.34%	0.74%	0.37%	-

(Receive)

Right Curve	Transmit					
	Truck total	Truck left	Truck right	Car 1	Car 2	Car 3
Truck	-	-	-	2.82%	3.39%	4.20%
Car 1	1.45%	5.13%	3.40%	-	0.25%	0.65%
Car 2	2.98%	5.77%	4.16%	0.27%	-	0.56%
Car 3	3.33%	6.23%	4.62%	0.51%	0.31%	-

(Receive)

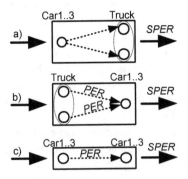

Fig. 5. Communication systems

Table 3. PER/SPER for RVM on the general road

	Average	Transmit					
		Truck total	Truck left	Truck right	Car 1	Car 2	Car 3
Receive	Truck	-	-	-	2.23%	1.60%	1.71%
	Car 1	1.84%	3.96%	5.19%	-	0.42%	0.76%
	Car 2	1.50%	2.92%	3.66%	0.49%	-	0.71%
	Car 3	1.62%	3.32%	3.36%	0.76%	0.39%	-

	Straight	Transmit					
		Truck total	Truck left	Truck right	Car 1	Car 2	Car 3
Receive	Truck	-	-	-	1.72%	1.28%	1.36%
	Car 1	2.12%	3.93%	5.32%	-	0.38%	0.71%
	Car 2	1.93%	3.22%	3.95%	0.50%	-	0.58%
	Car 3	1.86%	3.59%	3.62%	0.76%	0.32%	-

	Right Curve	Transmit					
		Truck total	Truck left	Truck right	Car 1	Car 2	Car 3
Receive	Truck	-	-	-	2.52%	1.65%	2.07%
	Car 1	1.51%	3.91%	4.24%	-	0.32%	0.72%
	Car 2	1.33%	2.97%	3.04%	0.44%	-	0.65%
	Car 3	1.43%	3.29%	2.77%	0.59%	0.42%	-

	Left Curve	Transmit					
		Truck total	Truck left	Truck right	Car 1	Car 2	Car 3
Receive	Truck	-	-	-	2.46%	1.88%	1.70%
	Car 1	1.89%	4.03%	6.03%	-	0.56%	0.84%
	Car 2	1.23%	2.55%	3.98%	0.53%	-	0.89%
	Car 3	1.56%	3.09%	3.70%	0.92%	0.43%	-

In the four result tables (Table1..4) the "Average" PER/SPER subtables are a un-weighted average of the scenarios (straight, curve etc.). This disregards the different duration of the scenarios. The other subtables (Straight, Right/Left Curve) show a weighted average over all three tested speeds, 50, 70 and 85 km/h. This implies that the average takes into account that more time was spent at slower speed. For each speed, one lap of the track was completed. For Table1 and 2 only "Right Curve" is applicable due to the geometry of the high speed circuit, i.e. only right curves and straights exist.

The top row of each subtable denotes the sender (TX) and left-most column de-notes the receiver (RX) in the communication pair. The white cells in tables denote PER, the others denote SPER. The three left-most columns in the subtables corres-pond to the b-configuration in Fig. 5. Here we can see the advantage of the redundan-cy scheme: The SPER (Truck total) is always lower than either individual left / right

PER. The first row in the subtables corresponds to the a-configuration in Fig. 5. Due to limitations in logging we can only see the SPER (i.e. PER is unknown) when the truck is receiver. The remaining quadrant corresponds to the c-configuration in Fig. 5, i.e. car receiving from car. We expected the PERs of the two directions of a communications pair, e.g. Car 1 to Car 2 and Car 2 to Car 1 to be more similar and cannot explain the difference.

Table 4. PER/SPER for roof antenna position on the general road

		Transmit					
	Average	Truck total	Truck left	Truck right	Car 1	Car 2	Car 3
Receive	Truck	-	-	-	3.31%	2.35%	3.58%
	Car 1	3.16%	6.73%	7.29%	-	0.55%	1.33%
	Car 2	2.48%	5.11%	5.72%	0.20%	-	1.00%
	Car 3	2.03%	5.35%	4.59%	*	0.05%	-

		Transmit					
	Straight	Truck total	Truck left	Truck right	Car 1	Car 2	Car 3
Receive	Truck	-	-	-	4.32%	2.99%	4.37%
	Car 1	2.30%	6.12%	7.35%	-	0.04%	0.50%
	Car 2	2.32%	5.45%	6.05%	0.75%	-	0.71%
	Car 3	1.99%	6.10%	5.34%	0.70%	0.10%	-

Right		Transmit					
Curve		Truck total	Truck left	Truck right	Car 1	Car 2	Car 3
Receive	Truck	-	-	-	3.41%	2.43%	1.91%
	Car 1	2.06%	5.49%	5.26%	-	0.51%	0.15%
	Car 2	1.65%	3.79%	3.57%	0.32%	-	0.04%
	Car 3	2.03%	4.42%	3.62%	1.00%	0.95%	-

Left		Transmit					
Curve		Truck total	Truck left	Truck right	Car 1	Car 2	Car 3
Receive	Truck	-	-	-	2.20%	1.62%	4.45%
	Car 1	5.11%	8.57%	9.24%	-	1.09%	3.33%
	Car 2	3.48%	6.10%	7.54%	*	-	2.26%
	Car 3	2.07%	5.52%	4.80%	*	1.21%	-

5.1   High Speed Circuit

Measurements on the high speed circuit, see Fig. 2, are categorized into Straight and Right curve driving and shown in respective subtables of Table 1 and 2. Constant speed is possible on the track; hence there are no accelerations or decelerations are assumed. During a lap of the high speed circuit approx. 20000, 14400 and 10000 packet are sent from each vehicle at each 50, 70 and 85 km/h respectively.

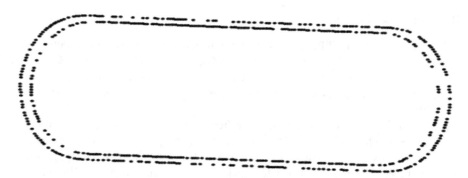

Fig. 6. Visualization of location of lost packets for RVM on the high speed circuit

Table 1 shows the PER and SPER for the truck and cars on the high speed circuit with the truck using roof antenna position. Table 2 shows corresponding but with the truck using RVM antenna position.

5.2   General Road

Measurements on the general road are categorized into Straight, Left and Right Curve and shown in the respective subtables of Table 3 and 4. The latter two is when the speed vector turns at 0.02 and -0.02 rad/s respectively. Constant speed is not possible; hence there are accelerations and decelerations along the track although these are not accounted for in the table. During a lap of the general road approx. 14800, 11200 and 9600 packets are sent from each vehicle at each 50, 70 and 85 km/h respectively. Table 3 and 4 shows the PER and SPER on the general road for RVM and roof antenna position respectively. * denotes lost measurements.

6   Analysis of Results

The test results from the measurements on the high speed circuit and general road are analysed in the following subsections. On the high speed circuit, the rear view mirror position performs better on average on the straights than the right curves. On the general road, the rear view mirror position performs better on average than roof antenna position on both straights and left and right curves. In both the general road and high speed circuit tests, the rear view mirror position was clearly superior to the roof antenna position on the truck and has more predictable performance. This can be seen in Table1..4. Note that a lower PER is better. We believe that this is due to the RVM antennas have more direct communication to the vehicles behind because the antennas are mounted further out from the center line of the truck than the roof antennas. The roof antennas are always obscured by the container and communication is multipath.

6.1   High Speed Circuit

Table 1 shows that the SPER and PER, for both left and right sending antenna, of Truck to Car x is always lower in curves for all speeds. Also, the SPER of Car x to Truck is almost always lower in curves. On average the roof antenna position performs better on the curves than the straights of the high speed circuit: 2.38% vs. 3.02% PER.

Table 2 shows that on straights, sending from truck left antenna to Car x always (i.e. at all speeds) has lower PER. On right curves, sending from the truck right antenna always has lower PER. The SPER of Truck to Car x has a weak tendency to increase in curves. The SPER of Car x to Truck is always higher in curves. On average RVM performs better on the straights than the curves of the high speed circuit: 2.04% vs. 2.65% PER. These averages are found by taking an unweighted average of PER (for all communication pairs) in the respective subtables (Straight and Curve). The same trends of differences between driving categories that can be seen in Table 2 (Straight and Curve) can also be seen at each speed.

Fig. 5 shows an outline of the high speed circuit that is drawn by the points where packets are lost. This is a visual correlation of platoon movement on track to loss of packets. The communication pair shown is from left and right antenna of the truck to Car 3. The speed is 70 km/h and direction of travel is clock-wise. On the two straights the PER from left and right is 2.0% and 4.7% respectively. On the two right curves the PER from left and right is 3.2% and 2.1% respectively. It can be seen visually in the figure that the density of the outer oval, i.e. lost packet from left, is somewhat greater the density of the inner oval, i.e. lost packet from right. Hence the "inner antenna" (right antenna) in the curve has lower PER. We believe that this is simply because in the curve the left antenna becomes more obscured with respect to the following vehicles, while the right antenna is more "in sight" of the following vehicles.

6.2   General Road

Table 3 and 4 show that on average RVM performs better that roof antenna position on both straights and left and right curve; 2.24%, 1.95% and 2.30% compared to 3.27%, 2.43% and 3.72% PER. This is found by taking an unweighted average of PER for all communication pairs (TX: Truck left/right, Car 1, 2 and 3; RX: Truck, Car 1, 2 and 3) in the respective subtables (Straight, Right and Left Curve).

The left RVM antenna on the truck mostly always has lowest PER in communication to cars (on average). With the roof antenna position on the truck the best side mostly corresponds to the direction of the curve, i.e. left curve implies the left side is better etc. As before, the effect of the curve geometry can be seen also on the roof antenna position.

7   Conclusions

The paper describes results of tests done on a V2V-communication system that was designed for the SARTRE vehicle platooning system. This is a cooperative application; that implies that communication between the vehicles is required to maintain operation. The performance of the V2V-system is studied according to PER and SPER. The paper draws general conclusions on the performance of V2V-communication and supports comparison of the tested antenna placements on the truck. In both the general road and high speed circuit tests, the rear view mirror antenna position was clearly superior to the roof antenna position on the truck and has more predictable performance. On average, the rear view mirror position performs better on the straights than the curves of the high speed circuit. On average, the rear view mirror position performs better that roof antenna position on both straights and left and right curves of the general road. We show that the curve geometry of the road affects which antenna of the truck has best communication to the following vehicles. In the platooning application that was studied, the "inner antenna" in a curve has the lower PER. The results in this paper can be used e.g. to support the design of communication protocol for cooperative vehicle applications.

Acknowledgments. The research leading to these results was received funding from the European Community's Seventh Framework Programme (FP7/2007-2013) under grant agreement n° 233683. SARTRE is a three year programme. Project Partners: Applus+ IDIADA, Institut für Kraftfahrzeuge Aachen (ika), Ricardo, SP Technical Research Institute of Sweden, Tecnalia, Volvo Cars, Volvo Technology.

At the time of measurements the main author, Carl Bergenhem, was employed at SP - Technical Research Institute of Sweden.

Support has also been provided by VINNOVA (Swedish Governmental Agency for Innovation Systems) FFI project RELCOMMH and EU FP7 project KARYON (grant agreement n° 288195).

References

[1] Karedal, J., Tufvesson, F., Abbas, T., Klemp, O., Paier, A., Bernadó, L., et al.: Radio channel measurements at street intersections for vehicle-to-vehicle safety applications. In: 2010 IEEE 71st Vehicular Technology Conference (VTC 2010 Spring), pp. 1–5 (2010)

[2] Bohm, A., Lidstrom, K., Jonsson, M., Larsson, T.: Evaluating CALM M5-based vehicle-to-vehicle communication in various road settings through field trials. In: 2010 IEEE 35th Conference on Local Computer Networks (LCN), pp. 613–620 (2010)

[3] Molisch, A., Tufvesson, F., Karedal, J., Mecklenbrauker, C.: A survey on vehicle-to-vehicle propagation channels. IEEE Wireless Communications 16, 12–22 (2009)

[4] Boban, M., Meireles, R., Barros, J., Steenkiste, P., Tonguz, O.: TVR-tall vehicle relaying in vehicular networks (2013)

[5] Campolo, C., Molinaro, A., Vinel, A., Zhang, Y.: Modeling prioritized broadcasting in multichannel vehicular networks. IEEE Transactions on Vehicular Technology 61, 687–701 (2012)

[6] Karlsson, K., Bergenhem, C., Hedin, E.: Field Measurements of IEEE 802.11 p Communication in NLOS Environments for a Platooning Application. In: 2012 IEEE Vehicular Technology Conference (VTC Fall), pp. 1–5 (2012)

[7] Bergenhem, C., Coelingh, E., Johansson, R., Tehrani, A.S.: V2V communication quality: measurements in a co-operative automotive platooning application. Presented at the SAE World Congress, Detroit, MI, USA (2014)

[8] Bergenhem, C., Huang, Q., Benmimoun, A., Robinson, T.: Challenges of platooning on public motorways. In: 17th World Congress on Intelligent Transport Systems, pp. 1–12 (2010)

[9] Bergenhem, C., Shladover, S., Coelingh, E., Englund, C., Tsugawa, S.: Overview of platooning systems. In: Proceedings of the 19th ITS World Congress, Vienna, Austria, October 22-26 (2012)

[10] Casimiro, A., Kaiser, J., Schiller, E., Costa, P., Parizi, J., Johansson, R., et al.: The KARYON Project: Predictable and Safe Coordination in Cooperative Vehicular Systems. In: 2nd Workshop on Open Resilient Human-Aware Cyber-Physical Systems, WORCS (2013)

[11] ETSI, Intelligent Transport Systems (ITS); Access layer specification for Intelligent Transport Systems operating in the 5 GHz frequency band ETSI EN 302 663 V1.2.1 (2013-07). In: Intelligent Transport Systems (ITS) (2013)

[12] IEEE Standard for Information technology, IEEE 802.11-2012 Telecommunications and information exchange between systems - Local and metropolitan area networks-Specific requirements - Part 11: Wireless LAN Medium Access Control (MAC) and Physical Layer (PHY) Specifications

[13] Strom, E.G.: On medium access and physical layer standards for cooperative intelligent transport systems in europe. Proceedings of the IEEE 99, 1183–1188 (2011)

[14] ETSI, Intelligent Transport Systems (ITS); Vehicular Communications; Basic Set of Applications; Part 2: Specification of Cooperative Awareness Basic Service; ETSI TS 102 637-2 V1.2.1 (2011-03). In: Intelligent Transport Systems (ITS) (2011)

[15] Bergenhem, C., Hedin, E., Skarin, D.: Vehicle-to-Vehicle Communication for a Platooning System. Procedia - Social and Behavioral Sciences 48, 1222–1233 (2012)

Reliability of Ad Hoc Networks
with Imperfect Nodes

Denis A. Migov[1] and Vladimir Shakhov[2]

[1] Institute of Computational Mathematics and Mathematical Geophysics SB RAS,
Prospect Akademika Lavrentjeva 6, 630090 Novosibirsk, Russia
mdinka@rav.sscc.ru
http://www.sscc.ru/
[2] Siberian State University of Telecommunication and Information Sciences,
Kirov Street 86, 630102 Novosibirsk, Russia
vladimir.shakhov@gmail.com
http://www.sibsutis.ru/

Abstract. In this paper we present a new network reliability measure
that is useful to evaluate performance of ad hoc networks with imperfect
nodes and perfectly reliable links. An ad hoc network is modeled as
undirected probabilistic graph. It is assumed that a network contains
initially excessive amount of nodes to provide properly functioning of
the network. That is, we consider the networks which carry on work
acceptably even if some amount of nodes fails. Nodes unavailability can
be caused by scuffing or intrusions. We define the reliability of such
network as the probability that sink nodes are connected and can collect
data from other nodes which amount exceeds a specified threshold limit.
The method for new reliability measure calculating is obtained. It is
shown that this method can be used for optimal sink nodes placement in
networks in order to obtain the most reliable version of network topology.
The provided approach can be used for performance analysis of attacks
against wireless sensor networks.

Keywords: ad hoc networks, wireless sensor networks, network reliability, random graph connectivity.

1 Introduction

The area of wireless ad hoc networks has received a lot of attention in the research community over the past several years. Research on generic wireless ad hoc networking also ramified to special types of networking like wireless mesh networks, wireless sensor networks, vehicular networks, radio frequency identification networks etc. In this paper we study a problem of reliability in these networks.

Probabilistic graph models have been used extensively in the literature for studying network reliability problems, especially in the case of unreliable edges [1–12].

M. Jonsson et al. (Eds.): MACOM 2014, LNCS 8715, pp. 49–58, 2014.
© Springer International Publishing Switzerland 2014

A case of unreliable nodes was a subject for studying too [13, 14]. However these studies do not usually take into account the specificity of wireless ad hoc network. The reliability of wireless sensor network with unreliable nodes was subject of study in [15]. In this research the reliability criterion is defined as all nodes connectivity. A method of sensors lifetime maximizing under required level of network reliability is offered. The reliability and survivability models for wireless sensor has been considered in [16]. Given these models, once can calculate the probability that a node is imperfect.

Some works [17, 18] have been proposed, in which area coverage reliability of wireless sensor networks is studied. In [19] the task of reliability of wireless distributed sensor networks is considered. Reliability is defined as the probability that there exists an operating communication path between the sink node (command node), and at least one operational sensor in a target cluster. A three-state node reliability model for sensor networks has been proposed in [20]. This model allows node to be in a state where only the wireless module is operating and a sensing module is failed. Thus, in this state a node can only relay traffic among its neighbours without generating its own data. The problem of events detecting with given level of reliability using the minimal number of network nodes is considered in [21].

In this paper we offer a novel concept of ad hoc network reliability, which has not been discussed in the previous works. We consider ad hoc networks with imperfect nodes and perfectly reliable links. Nodes unavailability can be caused by scuffing or intrusions. An operational probability is associated with every node. It is assumed that the node failures are statistically independent. At the same time, if any two operable nodes are within a communication range then the nodes communicate with each other without any losses.

A special feature of our model is that network contains initially excessive amount of nodes to provide proper functioning of the network. The failure of one or more nodes can cause the operational data sources to be disconnected from the data sink nodes (command nodes). However, operational nodes in the faulty nodes neighborhood may still be able to communicate with end-users, although, through a larger number of hops resulting in a larger delay of the information. For example, wireless sensor network may work acceptably even if some amount of nodes fails. In other words, it works until there is a sufficient number of workable nodes which are connected to any sink node. Another requirement for the network operation is the connectivity of sink nodes through workable nodes. We define the reliability of such network as probability of the proper functioning in the above meaning.

The rest of the paper is organized as follows. In section 2 the basic notations and definitions are presented. Sections 3, 4 describe the method of reliability calculation, section 5 describes numerical experiments which demonstrate optimal sink nodes placement in network. Section 6 is the brief conclusion.

2   Basic Definitions and Notations

We model the ad hoc network by an undirected probabilistic graph $G = (V, E)$ whose vertices represent the nodes and whose edges represent the links. We assume that each node succeeds or fails independently with an associated probability. Further on we refer to this probability as node reliability. We suppose that the links are perfectly reliable. We use following notations for the number of network elements: $|V| = N$, $|E| = M$. K — the specific set of nodes that correspond to the sink nodes of ad hoc network. Elements of this set we call terminals. It is assumed that K contains at least one element. As a rule, sink nodes are perfectly reliable. We have also an integer T such that $1 \leq T \leq N - |K|$. It is assumed that the ad hoc network is functioning properly if sink nodes are connected with each other and at least T nodes are workable and connected to any sink node.

Let us introduce some definitions. An elementary event Q is a special realization of the graph defined by existence or absence of each node. By V_Q we denote the set of all existing nodes in Q that are not sink nodes. The probability of an elementary event equals to the product of probabilities of existence of operational nodes times the product of probabilities of absence of faulty nodes. An elementary event Q is called successful if 1) all sink nodes are connected with each other by nodes from V_Q; 2) at least T nodes from V_Q are connected to any sink node. Otherwise, it is called unsuccessful.

An arbitrary event (an event is a union of elementary events) is called successful if it consists only of the successful elementary events.

An event is called unsuccessful if it consists only of the unsuccessful elementary events.

We define the reliability of the ad hoc network as the probability of the event consisting of all successful events and of them only. We denote it by $R_{K,T}(G)$. Further on, under the network reliability will be assumed this index, unless stated otherwise. In other words, the introduced reliability index is the probability that sink nodes are connected with each other and at least T nodes are workable and connected to any sink node.

It is obvious that problem of proposed reliability measure calculation is NP-hard since it includes the problem of k-terminal reliability calculation, which is known to be NP- hard [13].

3   Factoring Method for Network Reliability Calculation

Calculation of $R_{K,T}(G)$ may be done by the well-known factoring method [1,5,7] which has been modified for this purpose. This technique partitions the probability space into two sets, based on the success or failure of one network's particular element (node or link). The chosen element is called factored element. So we obtain two subgraphs, in one of them factored element is absolutely reliable (branch of contraction) and in second one factored element is absolutely unreliable that is, absence (branch of removal). The probability of the first event is equal to the reliability of factored element; the probability of the second event is equal to the failure probability of factored element. Thereafter obtained subgraphs are subjected to the same procedure. The law of total probability gives expression for the network reliability, in the general case for system S with unreliable elements it takes the following form:

$$R(S) = r_e R(S|e \ works) + (1 - r_e) R(S|e \ fails), \tag{1}$$

where $R(S)$ is the reliability of the S and $R(S|e \ works)$ is the reliability of the system S when the element e is in operation, $R(S|e \ fails)$ is the reliability of the system S when the element e is not in operation, r_e is reliability of element e. Figure 1 illustrates the factoring method for all-terminal reliability of graph G with unreliable edges. The corresponding formula takes the folowing form:

$$R(G) = p_e R(G_e^*) + (1 - p_e) R(G \backslash e), \tag{2}$$

where p_e — reliability of edge e, G_e^* — is a graph obtained by contracting edge e from G, $G \backslash e$ — is a graph obtained by deleting e from G. Recursion continues until either disconnected graph is obtained, or until a graph for which the probabilistic connectivity can be calculated directly is obtained — it can be a graph of a special type or small dimension graph [9].

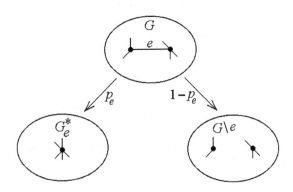

Fig. 1. Factoring procedure

Calculation of $R_{K,T}(G)$ may be performed in the same way, but it is more complicated because of the need to fulfill two conditions: the connectivity of terminals and the availability of a sufficient number of other nodes attached to them. It is convenient to choose as a factoring element one of the nodes adjacent to any terminal or the node adjacent to any already passed with reliability 1. Thus, it can be accumulating the number of nodes connected to chosen terminal. We keep the name "branch of contraction" and "branch of removal" despite the fact the process of contraction in graph is optional, as well as the process of removal. Let us consider separately the branch of contraction and the branch of removal of such process.

Branch of Contraction. In this branch the number of nodes attached to the terminal is increasing. If its number reached T it is necessary to check connectivity of all terminals via absolutely reliable nodes. If the check is successful then a final subgraph is received which corresponds to a successful event. If the check is unsuccessful then further factoring procedure continues only in order to ensure connectivity of the terminals. In other words, we calculate the probability of terminals connectivity in graph with unreliable nodes. It is convenient to use the method [13] for this purpose.

Branch of Removal. In this branch the number of nodes which in the process of further factoring could potentially be absolutely reliable is decreasing. Therefore, the event corresponding to the graph obtained by this branch can be authentically unsuccessful due to the disconnectedness of terminals or impossibility of reaching the required number of nodes attached to the terminals. It is suitable initially to check the first condition, that is, check whether the terminals are connected via non-zero reliability nodes. If the check is successful then we should check the second condition: the number of pending nodes (with the reliability of 0 up to 1) should be sufficient to achieve the required number of nodes attached to the terminals, that is, the number T. If the pending nodes are just enough to ensure this condition, all they become absolutely reliable. Thus successful subevent fully stands out from the considering event. It remains only to take into account that in order to obtain probability of this event it is required to multiply the value of reliability of pending nodes.

4 Algorithm

We use following notations for an algorithm description. All graphs arising during the factoring are presented as the array of probabilities P, $P[i]$ — the probability that the node i is operational. The reliability of such graph is denoted as $R(P)$. The array of the nodes reliabilities corresponds to the initial graph G. Let us denote it as P_0. Let us introduce for each graph arised during the factoring the value x — the amount of the considered nodes and the value y — the of amount nodes reliably connected any terminal. We need the function $R_K(P)$ — function for calculating the probability of connectivity K terminals (calculation method for this is given in [13]). Also we need boolean function $Connectivity(P)$ — function for checking the connectivity of terminals via nodes with nonzero probability. Let S be the cardinality of V/K.

We assume that the terminals are absolutely reliable. Otherwise, on preliminary step the terminals became absolutely reliable, and the final obtained value of network reliability need to be multiplied by the initial values of the reliability of the terminals.

A recursive procedure $Factoring(P, x, y)$ is a factoring algorithm for calculating reliability of the graph corresponding to array P. The values of x and y depend on P, however, to avoid recovering each time with use of P, they are left as individual parameters. Thus, the relaibility of G, $R_{K,T}(G)$, is equal to $Factoring(P_0, 0, 0)$ value. $RContract$, $RRemoval$, p are private variables of

---

Algorithm

1: **function** FACTORING(P, x, y)
2:      $RContract \leftarrow 0$
3:      $RRemoval \leftarrow 0$
4:      $v \leftarrow$ **arbitrary node** : $P[v] > 0$, v **has adjacent node** $j : P[j] = 1$
5:      $p \leftarrow P[v]$ ▷ "Branch of contraction"
6:      $P[v] \leftarrow 1$
7:      $x \leftarrow x + 1$
8:      $y \leftarrow y + 1$
9:      **if** $y = T$ **then**
10:          $RContract \leftarrow p * R_K(P)$
11:      **else** $RContract \leftarrow p*\text{Factoring}(P, x, y)$
12:      **end if**
13:      $P[v] \leftarrow 0$ ▷ "Branch of removal"
14:      $y \leftarrow y - 1$
15:      **if** $Connectivity(P) = true$ **then**
16:          **if** $S - x + y = T$ **then**
17:              $RRemoval \leftarrow (1 - p) * \prod_{P[i]>0} P[i]$
18:          **else** $RRemoval \leftarrow (1 - p)*\text{Factoring}(P, x, y)$
19:          **end if**
20:      **else** $RRemoval \leftarrow 0$
21:      **end if**
22:      Return $RRContract + RRemoval$ ▷ "Final computations"
23: **end function**

---

the $Factoring(P, x, y)$ procedure, that is they are created for every start of this procedure.

As it mentioned above, the problem under consideration is NP-hard so exact algorithm demands enormous computational effort. Nevertheless, proposed algorithm can operate with medium scale ad hoc networks. For a large scale ones it is possible to adapt the technique proposed in [4,9]. This technique can handle with various reliability measures, including the proposed one. It allows to decide the feasibility of a given ad hoc network without performing exhaustive calculation of reliability.

5   Applications

The proposed approach can be applied for counteracting against intrusions in wireless sensor networks. Usually, a typical attack, such that jamming, duty cycle tampering, selective forwarding, black hole, Sybil and other, covers a part of network nodes. Therefore, other nodes are operable. In spite of degradation of collected information quality the network can work properly. Methods for attacks performance analysis have to take into account this fact.

Let us consider a battery exhausting attacks. It is a well known that a battery power is usually a scare component in wireless devices. It leads to sensor vulnerability for fast battery depletion. The effect can be caused by the relaxed jamming attack [16], spoofed packets flooding, malware etc. As result of the attack the sensors functionality can be violated. Therefore, networks node becomes potentially imperfect.

Let V be a set of sensors and X be a set of possible points x_i for additional sinks placement. Let $N(x_i)$ is a set of sensors within the range of x_i sink. It needs to improve the system survivability with minimal cost. The corresponding problem can be formulated as follows

$$\sum_i x_i \to \min,$$

$$|\cup N(x_i)| \geq T,$$

and $\forall i, j$ the path between i and j exists. The intermediated nodes of the path are taken from the set $V \cup X$. The proposed method allows to get the solution of the optimizing problem above.

6   Numerical Experiments

Let us show how the proposed algorithm works. The test problem was the problem of optimal sink nodes placement in ad hoc network with unreliable nodes in order to obtain the most reliable version. Fig.2 shows a 5×5 grid network topology that we analyzed, supposing that all sink nodes are perfectly reliable and reliabilities of the other nodes equal to each other. Our goal is to place in the nodes of this grid three sink nodes to maximize the probability of access to sinks for at least T of other nodes in the network with the condition of sinks connected to each other. Three values for the indicator T were considered: 10, 15, 20. For each value of T, the solution was searched for three values of node reliability: 0.1, 0.5, 0.9. We have solved this problem by exhaustive search of all combination of nodes; for each combination its reliability was calculated. The

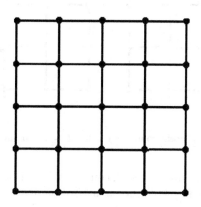

Fig. 2. Grid 5×5 topology

calculation time was about three hours; PC with Intel Core Duo 2,93 GHz was used for testing.

If $T = 15$, we have obtained different optimal sink nodes placements for different values of node reliability (fig. 3).

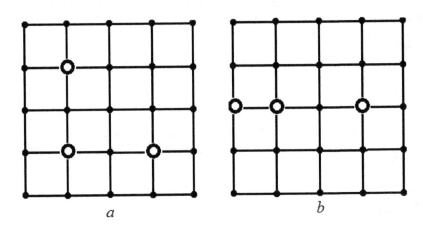

Fig. 3. Optimal sink nodes placements for $T = 15$ for $p = 0.1, 0.5$ (*a*) and for $p = 0, 9$ (*b*)

If $T = 10, 20$, optimal sink nodes placements were not different for different values of node reliability (fig. 4).

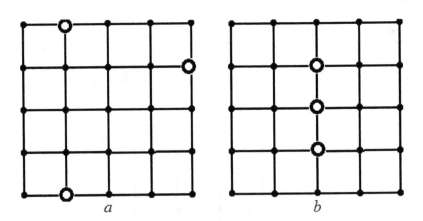

Fig. 4. Optimal sink nodes placements for $T = 20$ (*a*) and for $T = 10$ (*b*)

It is obvious that any sink nodes placement, which isomorphic to optimal, is optimal, too. For both placements shown in fig. 3 there are 4 isomorphic combinations of nodes. The placement shown in fig. 4 (*a*) has 32 isomorphic combinations and the placement shown in fig. 4 (*b*) has 2 isomorphic combinations.

7   Conclusion

This study proposes new reliability concept, which is applicable for analysis of ad hoc networks, in particular wireless sensor networks. The traditional concept of reliability (k-terminal network reliability) was taken as a basis of the proposed reliability rate. At the same time important features, which are typical for ad hoc networks, were taken into account. These are unreliable nodes and its excess amount for the network proper operation.

This reliability index could be used as the basis for other reliability indices, which are more completely describing the subject areas. For example, the restriction on diameter of a network makes such reliability index is more interesting from the point of view of practical applications, but also makes it more difficult to calculate. We can remove the requirement for sink nodes connectivity. Lack of this requirement is typical for networks in which sink nodes connect with the base station directly and independently. The methods for calculating the reliability with mentioned changes will not be radically different from the method proposed in this work. The problem of precise computing of these characteristics will be NP-hard. However, with help of method from [4,9] it is possible within a reasonable time to obtain the lower and upper network reliability bounds and make a decision about the reliability (or unreliability) of the network with respect to a given threshold. It allows us to solve some optimizational problems, such as the sink nodes location in ad hoc networks. An attractive potential area of proposed technique using is wireless sensor networks security.

Acknowledgments. This research was supported by grants of the Russian Foundation for Basic Research under Grants 14-07-31069, 14-07-00769.

References

1. Colbourn, C.J.: The combinatorics of network reliability. Oxford University Press, New York (1987)
2. Petingi, L.: Introduction of a New Network Reliability Model to Evaluate the Performance of Sensor Networks. International Journal of Mathematical Models and Methods in Applied Sciences 5(3), 577–585 (2011)
3. Khandani, E., Modiano, E., Abounadi, J., Zheng, L.: Reliability and Route Diversity in Wireless Networks. IEEE Tran. on Wireless Communications 7(12), 4772–4776 (2008)
4. Won, J.-M., Karray, F.: Cumulative Update of All-Terminal Reliability for Faster Feasibility Decision. IEEE Trans. on Reliability 59(3), 551–562 (2010)
5. Page, L.B., Perry, J.E.: A Practical Implementation of the Factoring Theorem for Network Reliability. IEEE Trans. on Reliability 37(3), 259–267 (1998)
6. Wood, R.K.: Triconnected Decomposition for Computing K–Terminal Network Reliability. Networks 19, 203–220 (1989)
7. : Moore E.F., Shannon C.E.: Reliable Circuits Using less Reliable Relays. J. Franclin Inst. 262(4b), 191–208 (1956)

8. Migov, D.A., Rodionova, O.K., Rodionov, A.S., Choo, H.: Network Probabilistic Connectivity: Using Node Cuts. In: Zhou, X., et al. (eds.) EUC Workshops 2006. LNCS, vol. 4097, pp. 702–709. Springer, Heidelberg (2006)

9. Rodionov, A.S., Migov, D.A., Rodionova, O.K.: Improvements in the Efficiency of Cumulative Updating of All-Terminal Network Reliability. IEEE Trans. on Reliability 61(2), 460–465 (2012)

10. Migov, D.A.: Computing Diameter Constrained Reliability of a Network with Junction Points. Automation and Remote Control 72(7), 1415–1419 (2011)

11. Rodionov, A.S., Nechunaeva, K.A.: Network Structure Optimization. Genetics Operators: Mutation and Crossover. In: ACM ICUIMC 2013, article 52. ACM, New York (2013)

12. Migov, D.A., Rodionova, O.K.: Calculating Two-Terminal Reliability in a Diameter Constrained Network with Cutenodes. In: ACM ICUIMC 2012, article 130. ACM, New York (2012)

13. Shooman, A.M., Kershenbaum, A.: Methods for Communication–Network Reliability Analysis: Probabilistic Graph Reduction. In: Reliability and Maintainability Symposium 1992, pp. 441–448. IEEEP Press, New York (1992)

14. Liu, S., Cheng, K., Liu, X.: Network Reliability with Node Failures. Networks 35(2), 109–117 (2000)

15. Shakhov, V.V., Choo, H.: Reliability of Wireless Sensor Network with Sleeping Nodes. In: Shi, Y., van Albada, G.D., Dongarra, J., Sloot, P.M.A. (eds.) ICCS 2007, Part IV. LNCS, vol. 4490, pp. 530–533. Springer, Heidelberg (2007)

16. Shakhov, V.V.: Protecting Wireless Sensor Networks from Energy Exhausting Attacks. In: Murgante, B., Misra, S., Carlini, M., Torre, C.M., Nguyen, H.-Q., Taniar, D., Apduhan, B.O., Gervasi, O. (eds.) ICCSA 2013, Part I. LNCS, vol. 7971, pp. 184–193. Springer, Heidelberg (2013)

17. Cai, W., Jin, X., Zhang, Y., Chen, K., Tang, J.: Research on Reliability Model of Large-Scale Wireless Sensor Networks. In: International Conference on Wireless Communications, Networking and Mobile Computing WiCOM 2006, pp. 1–4. IEEEP Press, New York (2006)

18. Shazly, M.H., Elmallah, E.S., Harms, J.J., AboElFotoh, H.M.F.: On area Coverage Reliability of Wireless Sensor Networks. In: IEEE Conference on Local Computer Networks LCN 2011, pp. 580–588. IEEEP Press, New York (2011)

19. AboElFotoh, H.M.F., Iyengar, S.S., Chakrabarty, K.: Computing Reliability and Message Delay for Cooperative Wireless Distributed Sensor Networks Subject to Random Failures. IEEE Trans. on Reliability 54(1), 145–155 (2005)

20. Shazly, M.H., Elmallah, E.S., AboElFotoh, H.M.F.: A Three–State Node Reliability Model for Sensor Networks. In: IEEE Global Telecommunications Conference GLOBECOM 2010, pp. 1–5. IEEEP Press, New York (2010)

21. Shakhov, V.V.: Experiment Design for Parameter Estimation in Sensing Models. In: Bianchi, G., Lyakhov, A., Khorov, E. (eds.) WiFlex 2013. LNCS, vol. 8072, pp. 151–158. Springer, Heidelberg (2013)

Reliability Enhancement for Hard Real-Time Communication in Industrial Packet-Switched Networks

Milad Ganjalizadeh, Magnus Jonsson, and Kristina Kunert

CERES – Centre for Research on Embedded Systems, Halmstad University
P.O. Box 823, SE-30118 Halmstad, Sweden
milad.ganjalizadeh@ericsson.com,
{magnus.jonsson,kristina.kunert}@hh.se

Abstract. Large industrial control and automation applications require reliable communication with strict timing constraints between distributed communication equipment. Packet-switched networks are widely used as a high-speed, deterministic, and low-cost solution to handle these types of distributed real-time systems. Although research on guaranteeing timing requirements in packet-switched networks has been done, communication reliability is still an open problem for hard real-time applications. In this paper, a framework for enhancing the reliability in multihop packet-switched networks is presented. Moreover, an admission control mechanism using a real-time analysis is suggested to provide deadline guarantees for hard real-time traffic. The performance evaluation of the proposed solution shows a possible enhancement of the message error rate by several orders of magnitude while the decrease in network utilization stays at a reasonable level.

Keywords: Distributed real-time systems, reliability, packet-switched network, hard real-time, industrial control.

1 Introduction

Nowadays, Ethernet (IEEE 802.3) is a popular choice for numerous industrial applications. Industrial Ethernet has, however, specific requirements, due to the nature of industrial applications and environmental conditions, making it different from corporate LAN. Real-time guarantees, which require precise synchronization between all communication devices, as well as a high level of reliability are the key parameters in the performance evaluation of different methods [1]. High bandwidth, high availability, reduced cost, support for open infrastructure, as well as a deterministic behavior make packet-switched networks suitable for a variety of different industrial distributed hard real-time applications. Examples of such applications include industrial automation process control systems, processing systems, and command and control systems.

There have been some approaches to guarantee the hard-real time deadlines in single-switch Ethernet. The most common solution is to let real-time traffic bypass the TCP/UDP/IP protocol, to avoid potential delays introduced by these protocols, and

M. Jonsson et al. (Eds.): MACOM 2014, LNCS 8715, pp. 59–74, 2014.

implement real-time scheduling with the real-time traffic being assigned top priority, such as in [2, 3]. These methods are unfit for large distributed networks since real-time scheduling is only provided for two hops. Providing real-time guarantees on spatially dispersed real-time embedded systems is complex since packets traverse multiple hops and it is necessary to have information about queuing mechanisms and traffic handling for both nodes and switches en route. In [4, 5] guaranteed service has been achieved using First Come First Serve (FCFS) queuing over standard Ethernet. An Ethernet-based standard widely used in networked industrial automation is PROFINET IRT (Isochronous Real-Time) [6].

In the mentioned approaches, timeliness is the only performance measure studied to satisfy hard read-time tasks. However, message loss can have the same catastrophic impact as deadline misses do when dealing with real-time applications. The environmental conditions for industrial Ethernet are hugely different compared to the conditions in an office environment, due to vibration, temperature, power pollution, air pollution, magnetic disturbance, etc. [7]. Therefore, it is tough or sometimes impossible to meet the objective bit error rate (BER), specified in the IEEE 802.3 standard. The studies that have been done for reliability in industrial Ethernet, such as [7, 8], mostly concentrate on hardware redundancy to enhance reliability. In fact, they consider permanent failures as the only cause of packet loss and the suggested solutions can be classified as preventive methods, i.e., they try to avoid packet loss but have no solution in case a packet is lost during transmission. In [9], packet loss has been considered as a parameter that might occur due to buffer overflow in Ethernet switches, and the solution suggested aims to prevent this overflow by traffic shaping. Reliable industrial communication has been studied in the context of wireless sensor networks (WSNs) though, and has resulted e.g. in a novel retransmission scheme for industrial point-to-point real-time wireless communication presented in [10,11] and a similar method for predictable real-time communication using IEEE 802.15.4 described in [12,13].

In this paper, we present a framework for reliable real-time communication over packet-switched networks, e.g., implemented as an enhancement of switched Ethernet. The framework guarantees timely transmission of ordinary transmissions, while part of each link's capacity is allocated for acknowledgements and retransmissions, respectively. As shown, the framework can improve the reliability considerably.

The remainder of this paper is organized as follows: section 2 presents the system model containing the framework overview and protocol definitions. The admission control mechanism using the proposed real-time analysis is presented in section 3. In section 4, a performance analysis is presented and lessons learned are discussed. Finally, section 5 summarizes and concludes the paper.

2   System Model

In order to increase the reliability for distributed switched real-time networks, we propose the use of timely retransmissions. In real-time systems, retransmissions have to be implemented in such a way that not only the first transmission has the possibility to arrive at the destination before the message deadline, but also all retransmissions must be able to achieve the required delay bound. Therefore, it is proposed here to divide the original message deadline into two deadlines: the first one is considered as the deadline for the first (the ordinary) transmission, and the second one is the delay bound for one or several retransmission(s). This section describes message handling from the highest layer, where the task is produced, to the lowest layer, where the Ethernet packet is sent over the physical link.

The application layer in the end nodes produces task sets based on the requirements of the industrial application, resulting in periodic hard real-time data traffic. The digital bit stream from one sender to one receiver belonging to a certain task is called channel (or logical real-time channel) and the messages over one channel are divided into different packets. Each channel is denoted by $\tau_{sn,k}$ which represents the kth channel of source node sn and signifies a prespecified periodic tasks. According to this, $\max(k)$ in every source node is the number of channels, Q, originating from that source node.

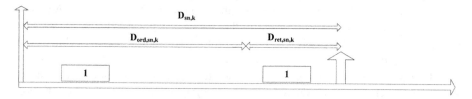

Fig. 1. End-to-end deadline division in order to enable timely retransmissions

In order to provide timely retransmissions, the end-to-end message deadline $D_{sn,k}$ is divided into two parts in the transport layer, as depicted in Fig. 1. The first part is the new deadline for the first (ordinary) packet transmission(s) of the message and the second part is the deadline for the packet retransmission(s) of the message in question in case of loss. This new ordinary deadline is valid for all packets per message. The division of deadlines is given by

$$D_{sn,k} = D_{ord,sn,k} + D_{ret,sn,k} \tag{1}$$

where $D_{ord,sn,k}$ and $D_{ret,sn,k}$ represent the end-to-end relative deadline for ordinary transmission and retransmission(s) in the transport layer, respectively.

The channel requested by the application layer is defined by $\tau_{T,sn,k} = \{dn, P_{T,sn,k}, D_{T,sn,k}, L_{T,sn,k}\}$, where T indicates the transport layer, dn is the destination node, $P_{sn,k}$ is the period, $D_{sn,k}$ is the total relative end-to-end deadline for the whole message to be delivered at dn, and $L_{sn,k}$ is the length of the message (in bytes).

The network layer handles path determination and logical addressing on the packet level, which necessitates certain changes to the channel definition. If $\tau_{N,sn,k}$ is the equivalent channel in the network layer N, it is represented as $\tau_{N,sn,k} = \{dn, P_{N,sn,k}, D_{N,sn,k}, L_{N,snk}\}$. All the parameters are the same as for the transport layer channel, but $D_{N,sn,k}$ is set to $D_{ord,sn,k}$ for the first transmission, i.e.,

$$D_{N,sn,k} = D_{ord,sn,k}. \tag{2}$$

The path between source and destination is assumed to be fixed in order to be able to perform a deterministic real-time scheduling. Consequently, all timing guarantees will be lost in case the routing of a channel changes. For the sake of simplicity, it is suggested here to add the static route as a channel descriptor in the network layer, i.e., $\tau_{N,sn,k} = \{dn, P_{N,sn,k}, D_{N,sn,k}, L_{N,snk}, S_{N,sn,k}, R_{N,sn,k}\}$, where $S_{N,sn,k}$ is the set of all switches between source sn and destination dn for the kth channel in sn. It is defined as

$$S_{N,sn,k} = \{(s_m, p_m)|(s_m, p_m) \in path\} \tag{3}$$

Switches are denoted by (s, p), representing a particular port p in a specific switch s which $\tau_{N,sn,k}$ passes through. As the route for a specific channel is assumed to be static, it can be given in the channel descriptor as an ordered pair (s_m, p_m), signifying that messages from channel $\tau_{N,sn,k}$ pass output port p of switch s in their mth hop. In other words, (s_m, p_m) is the source port for the point-to-point link in the mth hop of channel $\tau_{N,sn,k}$. The analysis presented in this paper is applicable for networks with different bandwidth over individual links. Accordingly, route $R_{N,sn,k}$ is defined as a set containing the bandwidth of all links used by $\tau_{N,sn,k}$. The mth member of this set is the bandwidth of the outgoing link connected to (s_m, p_m). From now on, the output port of the switch that is the source for point-to-point communication for the mth hop of $\tau_{N,sn,k}$ is represented by $S_{sn,k,m}$ and its bandwidth given by $R_{sn,k,m}$.

A set of tasks is said to be feasible if there exists a schedule in which all of them can meet their delay bounds [14]. Applied to logical RT channels, a set of channels is feasible if there is a schedule so that all of their periodic messages can meet their deadlines. In this paper, a novel admission control is proposed, including a feasibility check explained in the next section, which is used each time a new channel is requested. Its responsibility is to check whether the newly requested channel jeopardizes the deadline guarantees for the already accepted channels, or the new one, and the new channel is therefore only accepted if there are enough resources in both the source node and all switches en route. Hence, the complete path from source node to destination node has to perform the admission control done in the network layer. The admission control considers merely the ordinary deadline, i.e., the actual delay bound for the first transmission.

We propose an architecture (Fig. 2) where traffic, in descendant order of priority, is classified as follows: Acknowledgments, Retransmissions, Hard Real-Time traffic (HRT), Soft Real-Time traffic (SRT) and Non-Real-Time traffic (NRT). Hence, five different queues are used in each output port of both nodes and switches. Earliest Deadline First (EDF) queuing is utilized for acknowledgement, retransmission, HRT, as well as SRT queues, meaning that in these queues all packets are sorted according to their point-to-point absolute deadlines, NRT traffic is queued using FCFS. The reason to choose EDF is not only its developed and well-proven analysis framework [10], but also its optimality in uniprocessor scheduling in terms of feasibility [15]. The presented architecture uses strict priority queuing, i.e., packets in lower priority queues cannot be sent while there are packets in any of the higher priority queues. The only guaranteed traffic is HRT traffic, but both the acknowledgment queue and the retransmission queue are assigned higher priority to support shorter delays. In order to be able to implement real-time scheduling for the HRT traffic, flow control [16] for retransmission and acknowledgement traffic is introduced. A traffic shaper offering a specific service rate for each retransmission and acknowledgment queue will smooth this traffic and avoid starving the lower priority queues. Even though the queues using traffic shapers are guaranteed a prespecified capacity, this bandwidth can be used by lower priority queues in case no acknowledgements or retransmissions are queued. The traffic shaping mechanism eliminates bursty traffic for the two queues and leads to improved network performance [17].

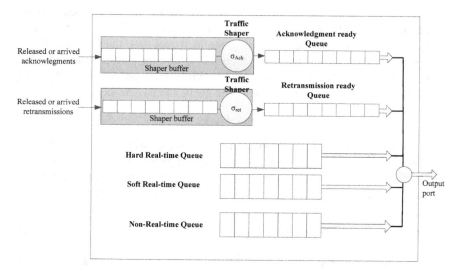

Fig. 2. Traffic classification in the proposed framework in all output ports

Without loss of generality, it is assumed that end nodes are aware of the traffic in intermediate switches. End-to-end channel establishment is proposed for ordinary transmissions, while point-to-point communication is suggested for acknowledgements and retransmissions.

3   Timing and Real-Time Analysis

3.1   Transmission Time

We denote the total transmission time (including headers, interpacket gaps etc.) of all packets belonging to a message of channel $\tau_{sn,k}$ as $T_{X\_tot,sn,k}$. The total transmission time for a full message of $\tau_{sn,k}$ in (s,p), which is presented as $T_{X\_tot,sn,k,s,p}$, is directly proportional to the ratio of the source node's send rate to the port's send rate, and can be calculated as

$$T_{X\_tot,sn,k,s,p} = \frac{R_{sn}}{R_{s,p}} \cdot T_{X\_tot,sn,k} \tag{4}$$

where R_{sn} and $R_{s,p}$ are the bit rates of the link of source node sn and switch port (s,p), respectively. It is worth noting that the scaling in the above equation for the whole transmission time of a message is also valid for the interpacket gap. According to the definition, the interpacket gap is the brief recovery time between packets. The minimum interpacket gap must be the amount of time required to send 12 bytes of raw data, which can be scaled relatively to the bit rate of the source node or the port.

3.2   Traffic Shapers and Their Influence on HRT Traffic

The objective with using traffic shapers is to force retransmission and acknowledgment queues to comply with a specific minimum interarrival time on the output stream, which makes real-time scheduling for hard real-time queues possible. As shown in Fig. 2, each traffic shaper has a buffer for arriving traffic. The shaper will smooth this traffic according to given traffic specifications, and send it to the ready queue. The traffic shaper for the retransmission queue can be denoted as

$$\sigma_{ret} = \{r_{ret}, P_{ret}\} \tag{5}$$

where r_{ret} is the bandwidth allocated for retransmissions and P_{ret} is the period or time interval during which r_{ret} is counted. The release pattern from the retransmission queue, using the traffic shaper, can be modeled as an arrival function and, hence, the worst-case arrival function $\alpha_{ret}(t)$ for the retransmission queue is given by

$$\alpha_{ret}(t) = \left\lceil \frac{t}{P_{ret}} \right\rceil, \forall t \geq 0 \tag{6}$$

The arrival function defines the number of times the traffic shaper has allowed retransmissions to leave the shaper's buffer and enter the ready queue (see Fig. 2), starting from $t = 0$ until a certain point in time. Therefore, the amount of retransmission traffic per period has to be specified. Given the bandwidth allocated to the retransmission queue r_{ret} and the whole bandwidth of a link R_l, the worst-case transmission time for retransmissions per P_{ret} can be calculated as

$$T_{wc,ret} = \frac{r_{ret}}{R_l} \cdot P_{ret} \cdot \tag{7}$$

$T_{wc,ret}$ is the maximum time per period during which the retransmission queue is allowed to send its packets. The worst-case amount of time that retransmissions have utilized the link to retransmit erroneous packets before a certain point in time t can therefore be defined as the Demand Function for retransmissions (DF_{ret}) and is calculated as

$$DF_{ret}(t) = \alpha_{ret}(t) \cdot T_{wc,ret}, \forall t \geq 0. \tag{8}$$

$DF_{ret}(t)$ is the worst-case transmission time that is considered for retransmissions in the real-time scheduling analysis of HRT traffic.

In the worst-case situation, all packets in the retransmission queue have the maximum packet size. In this case, the shortest possible period $P_{ret,min}$ for traffic shapers of retransmission queues to be able to send at least one full-size packet in each period is given by

$$P_{ret,min} = \frac{R_l}{r_{ret}} \cdot T_X \tag{9}$$

where T_X denotes the transmission time of a full-size packet. It is worth noting that when substituting P_{ret} in (7) by $P_{ret,min}$, the worst-case transmission time per period is T_X, which in fact was the objective when defining a minimum possible period. It is assumed that P_{ret} is set to $P_{ret,min}$, as the demand function in that case can be mathematically proven to have values always less than or equal to the demand function with P_{ret} set to any arbitrary value. This reduction in the demand function decreases the degree of pessimism in the real-time scheduling analysis.

The traffic shaper σ_{Ack} at the acknowledgment queue is defined by

$$\sigma_{Ack} = \{r_{Ack}, P_{Ack}\} \tag{10}$$

where r_{Ack} is the bandwidth allocated to the acknowledgment queue and P_{Ack} is the time interval or period during which r_{Ack} is counted. As acknowledgment packets are significantly shorter than normal data packets, a similar analysis for acknowledgments as given for retransmissions leads to a short P_{Ack}. Assuming the shortest possible packet for acknowledgments, and using (9) for acknowledgments, $P_{Ack,min}$ would become very short. Assuming further nonpreemptive transmission of packets, acknowledgements frequently would become blocked as lower priority packets already have been sent to the Network Interface Card (NIC). Therefore, it is suggested here to choose the same period for both shapers in the two highest priority queues, i.e.,

$$P_{Ack} = P_{ret} = P_{ret,min} \tag{11}$$

Accordingly, the arrival function for acknowledgments becomes the same as (6). Respecting r_{Ack}, a number of acknowledgments must be sent to comply with the traffic specification of σ_{Ack}. The worst-case transmission time for acknowledgments in each period is dependent on its bandwidth allocation and can be calculated as follows

$$T_{wc,Ack} = \left(\frac{r_{Ack}}{R_l}\right) \cdot P_{ret} + T_{Ack}. \tag{12}$$

The reason to add one T_{Ack} lies in the size of the acknowledgment packets. Traffic shapers check the amount of data that is sent by the acknowledgment queue during each period. As the last acknowledgement transmission can start close to the end of an interval of length $\left(\frac{r_{Ack}}{R_l}\right) \cdot P_{ret}$, the used time might exceed the amount specified. The demand function for acknowledgment traffic is given by

$$DF_{Ack}(t) = \alpha_{ret}(t) \cdot T_{wc,Ack}, \forall t \geq 0 \tag{13}$$

3.3   Real-Time Schedulability Analysis

According to (1), $D_{ord,sn,k}$ is the maximum end-to-end relative deadline for ordinary transmissions and corresponds to the delay bound for a complete message to arrive at the destination node and its acknowledgments to return to the corresponding source node. As ordinary transmissions of HRT traffic are the only guaranteed traffic, all delays must be subtracted from $D_{ord,sn,k}$ to isolate the end-to-end queuing delay for each end-to-end channel. The analysis tests if all the derived queuing delays, including the transmission time of the messages, can be guaranteed [10, 12, 18].

To isolate the pure end-to-end queuing delay, all other delays at the source and destination must be subtracted from the end-to-end deadline, resulting in the maximum end-to-end queuing delay $d_{e2e,ord,sn,k}$ for channel $\tau_{sn,k}$ with N switches en route and is calculated as

$$
\begin{aligned}
d_{e2e,ord,sn,k} = D_{ord,sn,k} &- 2 \cdot (N+1) \cdot T_{prop} - T_{e2e,block,sn,k} - T_{proc,source} \\
&- T_{proc,dest} - 2 \cdot N \cdot T_{switch} - D_{e2e,Ack,sn,k} - T_{margin} \\
&- T_{proc,ret}
\end{aligned}
\tag{14}
$$

where T_{prop} is the propagation delay and $2 \cdot (N+1)$ instances of the propagation delay are considered as both data packet and acknowledgement packet experience delay over $(N+1)$ hops. T_{margin} is a short interval of time included to cover for unexpected occurrences that can postpone the arrival of acknowledgments. The time required for packet checking and header checking to forward the packet to the right output port through the switching fabric is denoted as T_{switch}, and this delay is experienced in all N switches along the path for both data packet and acknowledgement packet. It will take a short amount of time for the source node to process the acknowledgment, $T_{proc,source}$, to initiate the retransmission, $T_{proc,ret}$, and for the destination node to process the received packet and prepare an acknowledgement, $T_{proc,dest}$. $T_{e2e,block,sn,k}$ is the end-to-end worst-case blocking time that a packet might suffer on its way to the destination due to nonpreemptive transmissions of packets. It can be formulated as

$$
T_{e2e,block,sn,k} = T_{X,sn} + \sum_{\forall (s,p) \in \tau_{sn,k}} T_{X,s,p}
\tag{15}
$$

The sum in (15) refers to all the maximum transmission times in all the ports that the packets pertaining to channel $\tau_{sn,k}$ pass. Finally, $D_{e2e,Acksn,k}$ in (14) refers to the maximum relative delay bound for the transmission of an acknowledgment. The mechanism to choose this delay bound is dependent on the characteristics of σ_{Ack} for traffic shapers (see (10)). The delay bound for acknowledgments is assumed to be $T_{wc,Ack}$ for each hop (see (12)). This implies that each acknowledgment is supposed to experience a maximum queuing delay of length $T_{wc,Ack}$, including its transmission time. Meeting this requirement is the performance measure of the acknowledgment traffic shaper. If enough resources are allocated to σ_{Ack} in regard to r_{Ack}, this requirement can be met. Therefore, the distributed model for (12) to achieve $D_{e2e,Ack,sn,k}$ can be rephrased as

$$D_{e2e,Ack,sn,k} = T_{wc,Ack,sn} + \sum_{\forall (s,p) \in \tau_{sn,k}} T_{wc,Ack,s,p} \qquad (16)$$

where $T_{wc,Ack,sn}$ refers to (12) in the source node sn and the sum includes the worst-case transmission times for σ_{Ack} for all (s,p) in the route of $\tau_{sn,k}$. The time-out time $T_{time-out,sn,k}$ after which the source node stops waiting for an acknowledgement and initiates a retransmission can be calculated as

$$T_{time-out,sn,k} = D_{ord,sn,k} - T_{proc,ret} . \qquad (17)$$

The queuing delay for each hop is specified directly proportional to its send rate. Different weights can be assigned to each specific hop if links have different capacities. The higher bandwidth a link has, the lower weight is assigned to it. The maximum point-to-point queuing delay at the nth hop, $d_{ord,sn,k,n}$, for channel $\tau_{sn,k}$ is calculated as

$$d_{ord,sn,k,n} = \frac{w_n}{\sum_m w_m} \cdot d_{e2e,ord,sn,k} \qquad (18)$$

where w_n is the weight assigned to hop n. The sum includes all the hops on the path of the channel in question.

As packets will arrive at different times after the first hop, jitter is introduced into the system. In order to ensure packet eligibility periodic in each hop, Jitter Earliest-Due-Date (jitter-EDD) [19] is suggested to resolve this issue. The proposed framework assumes that each packet is held at every hop for the interval of time between its actual arrival time and the theoretically calculated point-to-point queuing delay.

A real-time scheduling analysis is utilized to check if each HRT channel over the multihop-switched network can be guaranteed to meet its end-to-end queuing delay and also has the possibility of retransmissions. The analysis encompasses both necessary and sufficient conditions. The first, necessary but not sufficient, condition is a utilization check on each link over which messages from $\tau_{sn,k}$ are sent and simply checks whether the utilization of any link exceeds 100% in case a new RT channel is accepted. The utilization U_{sn} by source node sn must be equal or less than one, i.e.,

$$U_{sn} = \frac{T_{wc,Ack,sn}}{P_{ret,sn}} + \frac{T_{wc,ret,sn}}{P_{ret,sn}} + \sum_{\forall k \in [1,Q]} \frac{T_{X\_tot,sn,k}}{P_{sn,k}} \leq 1 \qquad (19)$$

where $T_{wc,Ack,sn}$ and $T_{wc,ret,sn}$ are given by (7) and (12), respectively, but in a specific source node sn. $P_{ret,sn}$ is chosen according to (9) for sn and $T_{X\_tot,sn,k}$, as the transmission time of a message from source node sn, is calculated according to (4). The utilization check must be done for all output ports on the path of $\tau_{sn,k}$, and in its calculation of the utilization it will include the ports for each channel that has this specific (s,p) in its path. The utilization function for (s,p) becomes as follows:

$$U_{s,p} = \frac{T_{wc,Ack,s,p}}{P_{ret}} + \frac{T_{wc,ret,s,p}}{P_{ret}} + \sum_{\forall (sn,k)|(s,p) \in \Gamma_{sn,k}} \frac{T_{X\_tot,sn,k,s,p}}{P_{sn,k}} \leq 1 \qquad (20)$$

where $T_{wc,Ack,s,p}$ and $T_{wc,ret,s,p}$ are defined equivalently to (19), but specifically for (s,p), and $T_{X\_tot,sn,k,s,p}$ is given by (4).

The second, sufficient, condition involves the workload function, which describes the complete transmission time for all messages (with an absolute deadline before a certain point in time t) pertaining to all channels over one link up to time t. The workload function assumes that all the channels start their period simultaneously, as this case was proven to constitute the worst case in terms of workload [20-22]. Acknowledgments and retransmissions, which can be seen as point-to-point channels, are also assumed to be released simultaneously at the beginning of their period, P_{ret}, with their worst case transmission times being $T_{wc,Ack}$ and $T_{wc,ret}$, respectively. However, this case will never occur in reality as acknowledgements are released when a packet arrives at a destination, and retransmissions are sent after a time-out interval, $T_{time-out,sn,k}$. Obviously, the worst-case assumption in this case introduces a certain amount of pessimism into the real-time analysis. Anyway, the workload function $h_{sn}(t)$ for source node sn is given by

$$h_{sn}(t) = DF_{Ack,sn}(t) + DF_{ret,sn}(t)$$
$$+ \sum_{\substack{\forall k \in [1,Q] \\ t \geq d_{ord,sn,k,1}}} \left(1 + \left\lfloor \frac{t - d_{ord,sn,k,1}}{P_{sn,k}} \right\rfloor\right) \cdot T_{X\_tot,sn,k} \tag{21}$$

where $DF_{Ack,sn}(t)$ and $DF_{ret,sn}(t)$ are defined in (13) and (8), respectively, but must be applied for the corresponding source node. Due to the assumption of jitter-EDD, packets might be kept in intermediary switches before becoming eligible for further transmission in order to ensure their periodic behaviour. Hence, the workload function can be calculated for intermediary switches as follows

$$h_{s,p}(t) = DF_{Ack,s,p}(t) + DF_{ret,s,p}(t)$$
$$+ \sum_{\substack{\forall (sn,k) | (s,p) \in \Gamma_{sn,k} \\ t \geq d_{ord,sn,k,n}}} \left(1 + \left\lfloor \frac{t - d_{ord,sn,k,n}}{P_{sn,k}} \right\rfloor\right) \cdot T_{X\_tot,sn,k,s,p} \tag{22}$$

where $DF_{Ack,sn}(t)$ and $DF_{ret,sn}(t)$ have to be applied for the corresponding (s,p). The first two terms in (21) and (22) calculate the workload introduced by acknowledgments and retransmissions. The simple condition for the workload function to test the feasibility of the scheduling is introduced in [20-22] and checks if $h_{sn}(t) \leq t$ or $h_{s,p}(t) \leq t, \forall t$, respectively. Due to the complexity caused by the introduction of continuous time, [23] proposed to perform the feasibility test at discrete points in time when deadlines occur, and upper-bound the values of t for which to test. Those adaptions make it computationally possible to implement this feasibility check.

4   Performance Analysis

For the validation of the proposed retransmission scheme and assessment of its performance in improving the message error rate (MER), a MATLAB simulator has been implemented in two levels: a channel-level simulator used for the schedulability analysis, and a packet-level simulator to simulate each individual packet over the network. The following metrics are intended to showcase the advantages and drawbacks of the proposed framework later in this chapter.

Definition 1. The network utilization, U_{Net}, for a set of accepted HRT channels, $\Gamma = \{\tau_{1,1}, ..., \tau_{1,k_1}, \tau_{2,1}, ..., \tau_{2,k_2}, ...\}$, is the average utilization of all communication links for a specific number of requested channels as calculated in (19) and (20). The acknowledgement and retransmission bandwidth is excluded for the case when using the presented retransmission scheme.

Definition 2. The MER for the set of accepted HRT channels is the ratio between the number of messages containing at least one packet that has not, or not correctly, arrived at the destination with respect to its timing requirement, and the number of produced messages.

In order to be able to conduct a study on the presented framework on packet-switched networks, certain assumptions were made:

- A linear network topology with three intermediary switches is chosen.
- The network contains ten end nodes. Switch 1 and 3 are connected to four end nodes, while switch 2 is connected to two end nodes.
- The bit rate over each full-duplex link is 100 Mb/s in each direction.
- The propagation delay for one hop (T_{prop}) is assumed to be 0.5 µs, corresponding to a link length of 100-150 m depending on the physical medium.
- The maximum packet size is 1542 bytes, the acknowledgment size 84 bytes. Correspondingly, the transmission time for a maximum sized packet or an acknowledgment is 124 µs and 7 µs, respectively.
- The parameters T_{margin}, $T_{proc,source}$, $T_{proc,dest}$, $T_{proc,ret}$, and T_{switch} in (14) are assumed to be negligible.
- The BER for each hop is assumed to be 10^{-7}.
- The $D_{ret,sn,k}$, in (1) is considered to be identical for all accepted HRT channels $\tau_{sn,k}$ and denoted as D_{ret} in this context.

The traffic is chosen randomly with discrete uniform distribution from Table 1. Additionally, each channel is assigned a random source and destination, also here using a discrete uniform distribution. In case of receiving the same source and destination node, the procedure is repeated to achieve different nodes as source and destination.

Table 1. Traffic specification

Traffic Class	Period (µs)	Deadline (µs)	Nr of packets per message
1	2000	12000	2
2	4000	24000	2
3	8000	32000	4
4	16000	48000	4

In all figures, the x-axis indicates the number of requested channels. Due to the extended time frame of packet-level simulations, especially for large numbers of requested channels, simulations have been run for one channel and in the following increasing the number of requested channel by ten for each run. The resulting graphs are average values of ten individual simulation runs, each with a duration of 100 hyperperiods[1] of accepted real-time channels. Fig. 3 through Fig. 5 present the simulation results for three different cases of r_{Ack}, r_{ret}, and D_{ret}.

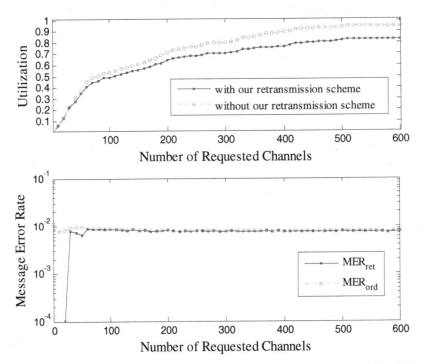

Fig. 3. Simulation results for the case of having $r_{Ack} = 4\ Mb/s$, $r_{ret} = 6\ Mb/s$ and $D_{ret} = 3000\ \mu s$

Fig. 3 presents the case of having $r_{Ack} = 4$ Mb/s, $r_{ret} = 6$ Mb/s, and $D_{ret} = 3000$ µs. As shown in all of the figures, the channel acceptance ratio for the case when having the retransmission scheme is constantly lower than for the case of not having retransmissions. At the saturation point in the utilization graph, the utilization penalty corresponds to a maximum of 12 percentage units. The MER graph presents the gain that is achieved for this penalty. There are two performance metrics presented in the MER graph: the MER for the case of not having any retransmissions (dotted line) and the MER when having retransmissions (continuous line). The first metric is measured while running the simulation assuming that there are no

---

[1] A hyperperiod is the least common multiple of all the involved periods.

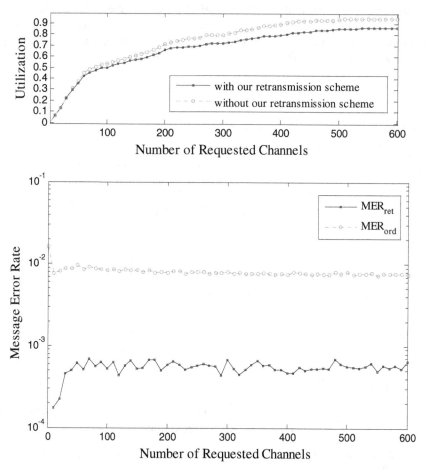

Fig. 4. Simulation results for the case of having $r_{Ack} = 6\,Mb/s$, $r_{ret} = 2\,Mb/s$ and $D_{ret} = 4000\,\mu s$

retransmissions present in the architecture, i.e., retransmissions are not counted. (Results when running the simulation separately, without implementing any retransmission scheme were very similar and are therefore omitted.)

Fig. 4 shows the results for $r_{Ack} = 6\,Mb/s$, $r_{ret} = 2\,Mb/s$ and $D_{ret} = 4000$ µs. Compared to the results in Fig. 3, there is a slight decrease in utilization penalty, while the reduction of MER in the case of using retransmissions lays around one order of magnitude in comparison to when having no retransmission scheme. The reason behind this difference in the MER improvement in Fig. 3 and Fig. 4 is the performance of the traffic shapers.

The results for the case of $r_{Ack} = 6\,Mb/s$, $r_{ret} = 6\,Mb/s$ and $D_{ret} = 4000$ µs are shown in Fig. 5. The utilization penalty at saturation is slightly higher as compared to Fig. 4. However, the improvement in MER is more than two orders of magnitude.

Obviously, the utilization does not dramatically change when varying the traffic shaper's bandwidth. The reason for that can be found in the linear nature of the network topology. The links connected to both sides of the switches reach 100% utilization faster and then no more HRT channels can be accepted.

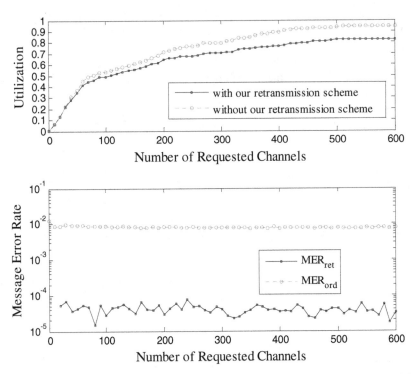

Fig. 5. The simulation results for the case of having $r_{Ack} = 6\,Mb/s$, $r_{ret} = 6\,Mb/s$ and $D_{ret} = 4000\,\mu s$

Assuming the packet error rate to be negligible, the number of packets sent from the source nodes is the same as the number of acknowledgments produced in the destination nodes. When the number of acknowledgments decreases, the experienced MER goes up. r_{Ack} must be chosen considering the size and number of acknowledgments compared to ordinary packets, i.e.,

$$\frac{T_{Ack}}{T_X} = \frac{r_{Ack}}{R} \tag{23}$$

where T_{Ack} and T_X are the transmission time for an acknowledgment and a maximum sized packet, respectively. r_{Ack} is the allocated send rate for the acknowledgement queue and R is the bit rate for the link. Given our simulation values and using (23), r_{Ack} has to be at least $5.64\,Mb/s$. This is the reason for not experiencing any improvement in MER for the case of $r_{Ack} = 4\,Mb/s$ in Fig. 3.

5   Conclusion

This paper summarizes a comprehensive and generic research study done to obtain more reliable packet-switched networks. A retransmission scheme is suggested to provide end-to-end retransmissions while still meeting the timing requirements of ordinary transmissions. The strict priority queuing, with a specific amount of bandwidth allocation through the use of traffic shapers for acknowledgments and retransmissions, is employed to fulfil the requirements of ordinary transmissions. Results show an improvement of the experienced message error rate by several orders of magnitude.

References

1. Sommer, J., Gunreben, S., Feller, F., Kohn, M., Mifdaoui, A., Sass, D., Scharf, J.: Ethernet – A Survey on its Fields of Application. IEEE Communications Surveys & Tutorials 12, 263–284 (2010)
2. Yiming, A., Eisaka, T.: A Switched Ethernet Protocol for Hard Real-Time Embedded System Applications. In: 19th International Conference on Advanced Information Networking and Applications (AINA 2005), vol. 2, pp. 41–44 (2005)
3. Hoang, H., Jonsson, M., Hagstrom, U., Kallerdahl, A.: Switched Real-Time Ethernet with Earliest Deadline First Scheduling Protocols and Traffic Handling. In: International Parallel and Distributed Processing Symposium (IPDPS 2002), 6 pages (2002)
4. Fan, X., Jonsson, M., Jonsson, J.: Guaranteed Real-Time Communication in Packet-Switched Networks with FCFS Queuing. Comput. Netw. 53, 400–417 (2009)
5. Fan, X., Jonsson, M.: Guaranteed Real-Time Services over Standard Switched Ethernet. In: IEEE Conference on Local Computer Networks (LCN) (2005)
6. Hanzalek, Z., Burget, P., Sucha, P.: Profinet IO IRT Message Scheduling With Temporal Constraints. IEEE Transactions on Industrial Informatics 6(3), 369–380 (2010)
7. Gong, Z., Liu, B., Yang, S., Gui, X.: Analysis of Industrial Ethernet's Reliability and real-time performance. In: 8th International Conference on Reliability, Maintainability and Safety (ICRMS 2009), pp. 1133–1136 (2009)
8. Lianzhi, G.: Reliability Study of Metro Ethernet. In: 5th International Conference on Computer Science and Education (ICCSE), pp. 1024–1027 (2010)
9. Wang, S., Shi, J., Sun, D., Tomovic, M.: Time Delay Oriented Reliability Analysis of Avionics Full Duplex Switched Ethernet. In: 8th IEEE Conference on Industrial Electronics and Applications (ICIEA), pp. 982–987 (2013)
10. Jonsson, M., Kunert, K.: Towards Reliable Wireless Industrial Communication with Real-Time Guarantees. IEEE Transactions on Industrial Informatics 5(4), 429–442 (2009)
11. Jonsson, M., Kunert, K.: Reliable Hard Real-Time Communication in Industrial and Embedded Systems. In: International Symposium on Industrial Embedded Systems (SIES 2008), pp. 184–191 (2008)
12. Kunert, K., Uhlemann, E., Jonsson, M.: Predictable Real-Time Communications with Improved Reliability for IEEE 802.15.4 based Industrial Networks. In: 2010 8th IEEE International Workshop on Factory Communication Systems (WFCS), pp. 13–22 (2010)
13. Kunert, K., Jonsson, M., Uhlemann, E.: Exploiting Time and Frequency Diversity in IEEE 802.15.4 Industrial Networks for Enhanced Reliability and Throughput. In: IEEE Conference on Emerging Technologies and Factory Automation (ETFA), pp. 1–9 (2010)

14. Hoang, H.: Enhancing the Performance of Distributed Real-time Systems. PhD Thesis, Chalmers University of Technology (2007)
15. Li, J., Xiong, M., Lee, V.C.S., Shu, L.C., Li, G.: Workload-Efficient Deadline and Period Assignment for Maintaining Temporal Consistency under EDF. IEEE Transactions on Computers 62, 1255–1268 (2013)
16. Wandeler, E., Maxiaguine, A., Thiele, L.: On the Use of Greedy Shapers in Real-Time Embedded Systems. ACM Trans. Embed. Comput. Syst. 11, 1–22 (2012)
17. Decotignie, J.-D.: Ethernet-based Real-Time and Industrial Communications. Proc. of the IEEE 93, 1102–1117 (2005)
18. Jonsson, M., Kunert, K., Bohm, A.: Increasing the Probability of Timely and Correct Message Delivery in Road Side Unit based Vehicular Communication. In: 15th International IEEE Conference on Intelligent Transportation Systems (ITSC), pp. 672–679 (2012)
19. Zhang, H.: Service Disciplines for Guaranteed Performance Service in Packet-Switching Networks. Proc. of the IEEE 83, 1374–1396 (1995)
20. Spuri, M.: Analysis of Deadline Scheduled Real-Time Systems. INRIA. Report no. 2772 (1996)
21. Baruah, S.K., Rosier, L.E., Howell, R.R.: Algorithms and Complexity Concerning the Preemptive Scheduling of Periodic, Real-Time Tasks on one Processor. Real-Time Syst. 2, 301–324 (1990)
22. Baruah, S.K., Mok, A.K., Rosier, L.E.: Preemptively Scheduling Hard-Real-Time Sporadic Tasks on One Processor. In: 11th Real-Time Systems Symposium, pp. 182–190 (1990)
23. Stankovic, J.A., Ramamritham, K., Spuri, M.: Deadline Scheduling for Real-Time Systems: EDF and Related Algorithms. Kluwer Academic Publishers (1998)

Modified Algorithm of Dynamic Frequency Hopping (DFH) in the IEEE 802.22 Standard

Denis Kleyko[2], Nikita Lyamin[1], and Evgeny Osipov[2]

[1] Halmstad University, Halmstad, Sweden
Nikita.Lyamin@hh.se
[2] Luleå University of Technology, Luleå, Sweden
{Denis.Kleyko,Evgeny.Osipov}@ltu.se

Abstract. IEEE 802.22 Cognitive Wireless Regional Area Networks is a first standard of wireless terrestrial system relying on cognitive radio concept and operating as an opportunistic system in the the vacant unoccupied frequency spaces of the licensed TV-frequency band. Concept of the proposed standard assumes special functionality to protect the operation of the primary licensed subscribers. Dynamic Frequency Hopping is the mechanism for providing connectionless operation of Wireless Regional Area Networks systems while ensuring protection of transmissions from the primary users. During its operation regular time gaps appear on the involved frequency channels. This paper introduces the concept of the efficient reuse of the vacant frequency resources appearing when using the Dynamic Frequency Hopping mode. The scheme for consecutive-parallel inclusion of the new Dynamic Frequency Hopping Communities-members in the Dynamic Frequency Hopping mode is presented. The proposed approach allows significantly decrease time of inclusion the new members into a new Dynamic Frequency Hopping Communities.

Keywords: IEEE 802.22 standard, Dynamic Frequency Hopping (DFH), WRAN, DFHC, DFH scheme.

1 Introduction

Limitations in number of available for communications frequency bands is a problem as number of various wireless systems grow rapidly. This makes researchers to focus on optimizing the utilization efficiency of the currently licensed bands. During the last decade investigation of opportunistic access approaches based on the usage of cognitive radio have been conducting [1]. In the opportunistic channel access approach secondary (unlicensed) users are equipped with cognitive radios, which allow them to transmit on the licensed bands while the primary users are inactive. The IEEE Work Group 802.22 (802.22 WG) proposed the first standard of the new wireless air interface [2], based on Cognitive Radio principle [3]. The IEEE 802.22 standard specifies the protocol for using the TV-frequency band by the secondary users. Globally, the standard uses band from 54 to 862 MHz. The network of devices allowed to use the TV band is referred as Wireless Regional Area Network or WRAN. A good overview of the standard is presented in [4]. The different aspects of the standard can be found in [2], [5], [6].

M. Jonsson et al. (Eds.): MACOM 2014, LNCS 8715, pp. 75–83, 2014.

In paper we propose the concept of using an unoccupied frequency resources, which appear in a typical DFH schemes [7] for increasing the number of active secondary users. It also presents the new Dynamic Frequency Hopping Community scheme. The main contribution of this article is that proposed approach allows more efficient parallel inclusion of several WRAN members into DFH schedule.

The paper is structured as follows. Section 2 provides state of the art. The DFH mode is described in Section 3. Section 4 presents the proposed approach for vacant frequency-time DFH resources usage. Modifications to the DFHC scheme are presented in Section 5. Finally, Section 6 concludes the paper.

2   Related Work

One of the key problems that is crucial for the IEEE 802.22 standard [8], [9] — the simultaneous satisfaction of two requirements: high quality of service (QoS) providing by WRAN services and reliable spectrum sensing for licensed subscribers protection. In [2] has been described the mechanism for reliable sensing in base operations mode using one frequency channel. It is defined to stop data transmission periodically, because spectrum sensing has to be performed during predefined time periods. To avoid connection interruptions the alternative operation mode named Dynamic Frequency Hopping (DFH) proposed for the IEEE 802.22 standard in [10]. In [11] using simulations it was shown that DFH mode can reduce the collision with incumbent users and achieve higher throughput. DFH mode allows both to transmit WRAN's data and to perform spectrum sensing simultaneously. To enable the effective frequency usage and avoid WRAN connection interruptions while spectrum sensing the so-called Dynamic Frequency Hopping Community (DFHC) was proposed in [7]. This approach assumes that several neighbor WRANs work in the DFH coordinated mode being organized in the DFHC. The main idea of DFHC is that neighboring WRANs are collaborating when assigning frequency channels for DFH and coordinate the execution of corresponding dynamic frequency hopping operations.

3   Dynamic Frequency Hopping (DFH)

The IEEE 802.22 standard defines that WRAN should continuously use a channel in the operating mode for no longer than 2 seconds. Between two subsequent operation phases WRAN must sense for the for the presence of licensed subscribers [2]. WRAN devices must be able to recognize digital TV signal (DTV) with levels up to -116 dB with maximum error probability equals of 0.1 [12]. The analysis of the well-known technologies shows that this procedure spends dozens of milliseconds per channel [13]. For example, DTV sensing on 6 MHz requires around 100 ms per channel. However, the IEEE 802.22 standard requires maximal delays to be less than 20 ms to provide satisfactory Quality of Service for delay sensitive applications such as VoIP [12]. Thus the it was proposed to apply DFH in the IEEE 802.22 [2]. WRAN in the DFH mode changes frequency channel for transmission among all available channels. Fig. 1 presents an example of DFH principle for the case of three WRANs.

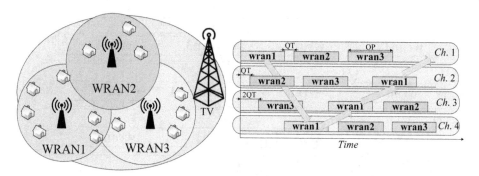

Fig. 1. An example of three WRANs

In DFH mode N WRANs operate under $N + 1$ vacant channels. Fig. 1 shows an operation of DFH phase shifting process [7], [2] for $N = 3$ neighbor WRANs over $N + 1 = 4$ available channels, where OP – operation phase is a time slot of fixed duration when WRAN transmits and receives data. Each WRAN shifts its DFH OPs on the QT — Quiet Time relatively to the shift of previous WRAN. QT intervals are used for a channel sensing. It means that QT must be not less than minimum time required for the reliable sensing. For instance, WRAN2 shifts the execution of its operation by one QT period relatively to WRAN1 operation, while WRAN3 by the one period, relatively to WRAN2. This approach allows to support continuous connection for every WRAN while preserve necessary sensing for incumbents presence to protect licenced subscribers.

Thus, the group of N interfering WRANs can operate over $N + 1$ channels as long as the duration of one operation phase is more than $N \cdot QT$.

4   The Proposed Approach for Vacant Frequency-Time DFH Resource Usage

The DFH scheme causes time gaps of $t_{vac} = OP - N * QT$ every $N * (OP + (QT - 1))$ due to the phase shifting operation. The interval between the first and the last WRANs in the DFH mode is much more than QT and it equals $t_{vac} = OP - 2QT$. We emphasize this vacant resource in Fig. 2 as "VACANT", taking into account two more sensing steps: after OP WRAN3 is finishing and before OP WRAN1 is starting.

We propose to use these vacant frequency-time resources for additional WRAN, which will operate with interruptions. This method can suit for the cases when one of the $N + 1$ channels is occupied by a licensed device. Then, WRAN with the lowest priority should switch to a mode with interruptions for the time when channel remains unavailable. Fig. 2 illustrates this example, demonstrating WRAN4 operating over vacant intervals.

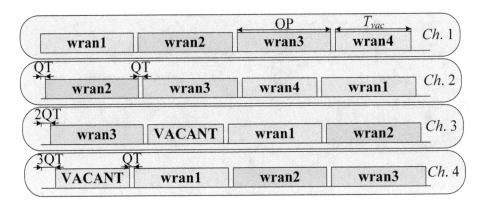

Fig. 2. Illustration of a vacant resources in the DFH phase shifting process

Generally, when one has N WRANs and $N + 1$ available channels, the vacant frequency-time slots, which appear in the group of channels, can be described within the expressions given below.

Time of the k-th operation phase beginning:

$$T_{start} = N \cdot QT + OP \cdot k. \tag{1}$$

Time of the k-th operation phase ending:

$$T_{end} = OP - QT + OP \cdot k = OP \cdot (k + 1) - QT. \tag{2}$$

Duration of the vacant operation phase (OP_{vac}) is then:

$$OP_{vac} = T_{end_k} - T_{start_k} = OP \cdot k + OP - QT - OP \cdot k - \\ - N \cdot QT = OP - (N + 1) \cdot QT. \tag{3}$$

The interruption time between transmissions:

$$QT_{vac} = T_{start_{k+1}} - T_{end_k} = N \cdot QT + OP \cdot (k + 1) - \\ - OP \cdot (k + 1) + QT = (N + 1) \cdot QT. \tag{4}$$

Therefore in vacant intervals, which appear in $N + 1$ channels in DFH mode, data transferring can be executed by one more WRAN. In this case, time of transferring in one interval is $OP_{vac} = OP - (N + 1) \cdot QT$, and connection interruption between operation intervals is $QT_{vac} = (N + 1) \cdot QT$.

5   Modifications to the DFHC Scheme

5.1   Dynamic Frequency Hopping Community

According to the definition proposed in [7], Dynamic Frequency Hopping Community — is a nonempty group of neighbor WRANs, which supplies coordinated DFH operations to avoid interference spectrum sensing. DFHC consists of one arbiter WRAN and usually several member WRANs. The *DFHC-arbiter* is responsible for maintaining the membership in the group, construction of DFH schedules and the distribution of that information to all members of the group. DFHC members provide all the necessary information about their neighbors and the available channels to the arbiter, i.e. sensing results and watch for neighbor WRAN channels utilization [7].

Every DFH schedule has its time to live (TTL hereinafter), which is counted and distributed by the arbiter. Each member can use the channel, constructed by the DFH scheduler, during this time. Arbiter periodically refreshes and broadcasts the information about the schedule to group's members. The new schedule starts right after the time when the previous one is completed. The new one's has to be confirmed by all the group members. If any member does not receive this information before the previous schedule is completed, it cannot operate anymore in the DFH mode and switches to the non-hopping operation mode.

In general, the updating of the scgedule can be organized in two ways: either by starting the new schedule when the TTL of the previous one has elapsed or by consecutive joining of all members to the new schedule [7].

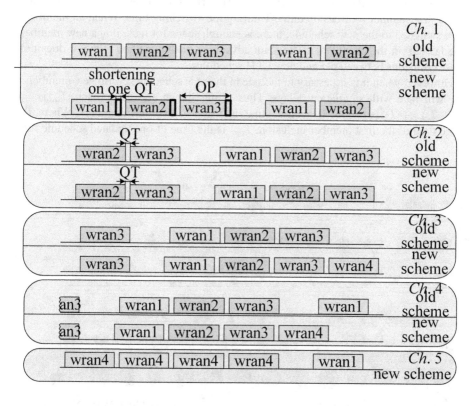

Fig. 3. Consecutive switching for inclusion of new DFHC-member

5.2 Shortcomings of the Standard Scheme for New DFHC-Members Inclusion

The first approach ensures collision avoidance during the schedule switching. Even if some of the group members do not get the information about the new model, they still cannot continue to operate by using the old schedule after TTL has expired. However, this approach is not flexible enough in terms of distribution of the new schedule during the execution time of the previous schedule. It could cause conflicts: if someone does not get the updated schedule and still works with the old one [7].

This problem can be avoided by using serial switching of DFH schedules. This method assumes inclusion of each member to the new schedule by the arbiter individually. Members are chosen from those, who are not yet scheduled. This allows to avoid collisions between the operating and new unscheduled devices. The arbiter checks whether WRANs are switched or not by sensing the channel. In this case, even if some members do not switch to the new schedule, all scheduled members can use the new model without causing any collisions [7].

Consider for example dynamic scheduling of the new DFHC-member as shown in Fig. 3 (old schedule is illustrated as well). At first, all members are switched to the new schedule. It means that their OPs shift on one QT period on channel 4. Additionally, OPs of the first channel shortens on one QT during the switching time. When all members have switched to the new schedule, there is enough space for including a new member (the last OP in the channel 4). The main advantage of this method is that it does not cause collisions between old and new DFH schedules.

However, when it is necessary to include in the new schedule several new members, one will face with significant delays. Thus, using shown above approach, $T_{add2} = T_1 + T_{cyc} + T_2$ is needed for consecutive inclusion of two new members. Where T_1 is the time of the first member inclusion, T_{cyc} is the time of one updated schedule full

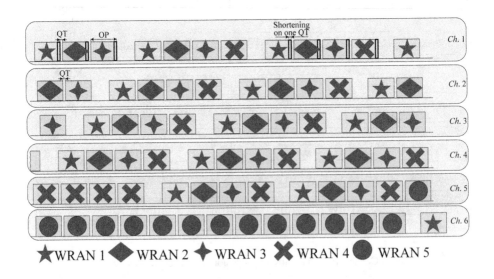

Fig. 4. Consecutive including of two new WRAN in a standard way

cycle, T_2 — time of the second member including. The shown above arguments, which are defined as follows:

$$T_1 = N \cdot (OP + QT). \tag{5}$$

$$T_2 = (N + 1) \cdot (OP + QT). \tag{6}$$

$$T_{cyc} = (N + 1) \cdot OP + t_{vac} - QT = (N + 1) \cdot OP + OP - \\ - (N - 1) \cdot QT - QT = (N + 2) \cdot OP - N \cdot QT. \tag{7}$$

Fig. 4 provides an example illustrating the consecutive inclusion of two new WRAN into the existing schedule takes considerable time. Also when the number of DFHC-members is increasing this value grows as well. Thus, if in Fig. 4 WRAN4 inclusion takes about 3 OP, WRAN5 takes more than 4 OP and so on. Besides, before each new member inclusion it is necessary to wait for the full schedule updating cycle. To optimize the WRAN inclusion process and decrees the inclusion delays we propose the consecutive-parallel scheme for the members inclusion in the following subsection.

5.3   Solution: Consecutive-Parallel Scheme of New DFHC-Members Inclusion

The core of the proposed method is that at the beginning all members of the DFHC shift their schedules on $K \cdot QT$ in one of channels (e.g. channel one in Fig. 5), where K is the number of new members, which must be included into the DFHC. The same way [7], in the first channel OPs are shorten on QT during inclusion time. Using this method, it is possible to decrease the inclusion time in comparison with the standard consecutive

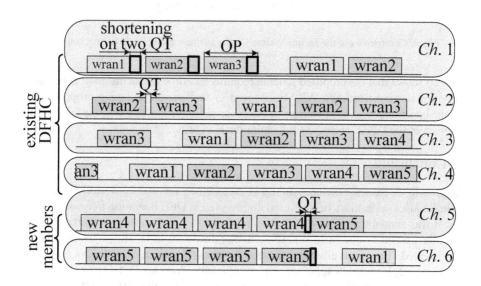

Fig. 5. Illustration of consecutive-parallel scheme for members switching

scheme (Fig. 3). Thereby time for the inclusion of the last new-added WRAN for the proposed consecutive-parallel scheme is determined as:

$$T_K = N \cdot (OP + QT) - QT. \tag{8}$$

An example for the consecutive-parallel inclusion of two new WRANs is shown in Fig. 5.

Comparison of the last new-added WRAN inclusion time for the standard scheme (5), (6), (7) and the prosed one (8) is shown in Fig. 6. The following parameters values were used during the estimation:

- Duration of one QT is 0.1 sec;
- Duration of one OP is 2 sec;
- Initial number of DFHC group members is 3.

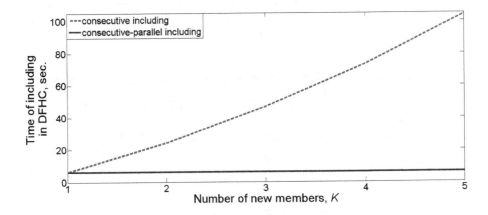

Fig. 6. Comparison of the inclusion time for the last new members in both schemes

Fig. 6 shows that the proposed scheme requires less time for inclusion of new members even starting from two WRANs. Moreover the time of inclusion proposed this scheme is permanent. Such behavior of the proposed algorithm is due to the fact that all members of the DFHC shift their schedules on $K \cdot QT$.

6   Conclusion

This article discussed efficiency of DFH mechanism for 802.22 WRAN. Standard scheme causes appearance of time gaps on involved in DFH operation frequency channels. It was shown that these resources can be used for operation with partly connection interruptions of one extra WRAN. Another drawback in DFHC inclusion scheme was detected. The more effective consecutive-parallel scheme of WRANs inclusion was proposed. Introduced approach may significantly decrease DFHC transition time. Thus, extensions proposed in the paper allow to increase the efficiency of DFH standard schemes within insignificant growth of complexity.

References

1. Ghasemi, A., Sousa, E.S.: Collaborative spectrum sensing for opportunistic access in fading environments. In: IEEE International Symposium on New Frontiers in Dynamic Spectrum Access Networks, DySPAN, pp. 131–136 (2005)
2. IEEE Std. 802.22-2011, Part 22: Cognitive Wireless RAN Medium Access Control (MAC) and Physical Layer (PHY) Specifications: Policies and Procedures for Operation in the TV Bands (July 2011)
3. Biglieri, E., Goldsmith, A.J., Greenstein, L.J., Mandayam, N.B., Vincent Poor, H.: Principles of Cognitive Radio. Cambridge University Press (2012)
4. Cordeiro, C., Challapali, K., Birru, D.: IEEE 802.22: An introduction to the first wireless standard based on cognitive radios. Journal of Communications 1(2), 38–47 (2006)
5. IEEE Std. 802.22-2012, Part 22.2: Installation and Deployment of IEEE 802.22 Systems (September 2012)
6. IEEE Std. 802.22-2010, Part 22.1: Standard to Enhance Harmful Interference Protection for Low-Power Licensed Devices Operating in TV Broadcast Bands (November 2010)
7. Hu, W., Willkomm, D., Abusubaih, M., Gross, J., Vlantis, G., Gerla, M., Wolisz, A.: Dynamic frequency hopping communities for efficient IEEE 802.22 operation. IEEE Communications Magazine 45, 80–87 (2007)
8. Al-Zubi, R., Hawa, M., Al-Sukkar, G., Darabkh, K.A.: Markov-Based Distributed Approach for mitigating melf-coexistence problem in IEEE 802.22 WRANs. The Computer Journal, 1–11 (August 2013)
9. De Domenico, A., Strinati, E.C., Di Benedetto, M.-G.: A survey on mac strategies for cognitive radio networks. IEEE Communications Surveys and Tutorials 14(1), 21–44 (2012)
10. Chu, L., et al.: 22-06-0113-01-0000 dynamic frequency hopping community. Tech. proposal submitted to IEEE 802.22 WG
11. Tong, J., Wu, H., Yin, C., Ma, Y., Li, J.: Dynamic frequency hopping vs. nonhopping in IEEE 802.22 systems. In: IEEE International Conference on Network Infrastructure and Digital Content, IC-NIDC, pp. 95–99 (2009)
12. Stevenson, C.R., Cordeiro, C., Sofer, E., Chouinard, G.: Functional requirements for the 802.22 WRAN standard r47 (2006)
13. Chouinard, G., Cabric, D., Gosh, M.: Sensing thresholds for the 802.22 WRAN standard r8

Fuzzy C-Means Clustering in Energy Detection for Cooperative Spectrum Sensing in Cognitive Radio System

Subhankar Chatterjee[1], Avik Banerjee[1],
Tamaghna Acharya[2], and Santi P. Maity[1]

[1] Department of Information Technology
[2] Department of Electronics and Telecommunication Engineering
Indian Institute of Engineering Science and Technology,
Shibpur, Howrah, India - 711103
subhankar.ece@gmail.com, avik_364@yahoo.in,
t_acharya@telecom.becs.ac.in, santipmaity@it.becs.ac.in

Abstract. An energy detection based cooperative spectrum sensing approach using Fuzzy c-means clustering is proposed in this work for cognitive radio system. The objective here is to categorize first the measured PU energy contents into multiple classes to highlight the relative degree in presence or absence of PU and Fuzzy c-means (FCM) algorithm is utilized for this purpose. A soft decision based spectrum sensing is proposed here to categorize the presence or absence of PU in four different classes which then develop individual binary decision functions. Resultant binary decision function is then developed using OR fusion rule. Simulation results highlight that the proposed scheme provides high detection probability at low diversity and less number of samples. The results are further compared with the performance of the conventional energy detector methods to highlight the significance of the proposed scheme.

Keywords: Cooperative Spectrum Sensing, Energy Detector, Cluster based sensing, Fuzzy c-means, Soft decision.

1 Introduction

In recent years, radio frequency spectrum scarcity has become a major concern due to the increased number of wireless devices with data intensive applications such as interactive and multimedia services. In traditional static spectrum allocation scheme, the available frequency spectrum is divided and allocated exclusively to specific service providers or users called licensed users or primary users. Most frequency bands being already allotted, it is therefore difficult to find empty spectrum for emerging wireless networks [6]. Moreover, the static frequency allocation leads to the spectrum under-utilization scenario as mentioned in the reports [3, 12], published by several regulatory bodies, e.g. Federal Communications Commission (FCC) in USA and Office of Communications

M. Jonsson et al. (Eds.): MACOM 2014, LNCS 8715, pp. 84–95, 2014.
© Springer International Publishing Switzerland 2014

(OFCOM) in UK. Cognitive radio (CR) concept has been developed as a tool to solve spectrum under-utilization and spectrum shortage problems. Cognitive radio users (CRUs) continuously sense the presence of licensed primary user (PUs). CR users can either opportunistically access the spectrum when it is not occupied by PU or share the specific spectrum with PU maintaining the interference to the latter below an interference temperature limit [6].

Spectral sensing, dynamic spectrum access, spectrum sharing, spectrum management and secondary transmission are few key research issues in CR systems. Spectrum sensing (SS) is the key research issue that highlights cognition capability and cognitive reconfigurability. Spectrum utilization information through reliable spectrum sensing (to detect PU activity) is necessary to be available at secondary users (SUs) to avoid unwanted interference to PU transmission. On the other hand, SS ensures better utilization of vacant radio spectrum (spectrum holes) improving SU transmission. SS performance is traditionally specified by two metrics: (i) probability of detection, which refers to the probability of finding PU's presence in a particular spectrum through spatio-temporal sensing when the spectrum is actually occupied by PU, and (ii) probability of false alarm, which represents the probability of the event that SU is deciding in favor of PU's presence, although the particular spectrum remains idle [1]. Several spectrum sensing techniques namely energy detection (ED), matched filtering (MF), cyclostationary feature detection (CS), generalized likelihood ratio test (GLRT) etc. are already reported in the literature with individuals having the relative merits and the demerits.

Among all these techniques, energy detection is found to be the simplest and the widely used spectrum sensing mechanism. It is the optimal sensing approach when there is no prior knowledge of PU signal. Energy detector senses the presence of PU signal by measuring the energy of the input signal over a specific time interval [9]. However, the performance of energy detector degrades in cases of low PU signal-to-noise ratio (SNR) and noise uncertainty. Matched filtering [13] and cyclostationary feature detectors [5] provide improved sensing performance in less sensing time and in low PU SNR scenarios, respectively. These approaches, unlike energy detection need to know certain features e.g. PU signal pattern, cyclic frequency of the PU signal, symbol rate, pilot signal etc.. It is also worth to mention that recent literature on cognitive radio spectrum sensing suggests the use of generalized likelihood ratio test (GLRT) [8], particularly at low SNR and in the situation when there is uncertainty in noise and signal power. However, parameter estimation in GLRT involves several complex computation and is not energy efficient always. More recent spectrum sensing techniques include wavelet based spectrum sensing [14], compressive sampling based spectrum sensing [4] etc. The first one aims to exploit multiresolution analysis for improvement in SS, while the later one allows detection at low measurement space with a scope of energy efficient system design.

The performance of non-cooperative SS degrades severely due to the effects of multipath fading, shadowing, receiver uncertainty issues in wireless channels. Cooperative spectrum sensing (CSS) [10, 17] has been shown to improve sensing performance of the cognitive radio system by exploiting the spatial diversity of the received PU signal at multiple SUs or single SU and relay node(s). The hard decision based CSS (either centralized or distributed) is well addressed in the literature to resolve binary hypothesis, about the presence or absence of PU in two classes. In traditional CSS, the sensing results of individual SU's are combined using maximum ratio combiner, selection combiner, equal gain combiner etc. Due to the uncertainty in propagation medium CSS may fail to offer desirable sensing result. Instead of conventional mathematical approaches fuzzy logic based soft decision approaches [11, 16, 18] are being explored as an alternative to reduce noise uncertainty that leads to improved SS even at low SNR. In [16], the performance of cooperative spectrum sensing is improved by evaluating the credibility of each SU using fuzzy comprehensive evaluation. The authors in [18] utilize two thresholds and fuzzy logic values (indicating sensing decisions) to improve sensing reliability and the bandwidth efficiency of the SU network. These works highlight the improved performance of the energy detector based CSS using fuzzy logic over the conventional energy detector based CSS. CSS may provide improved sensing performance exploiting spatial diversity but at the cost of an increase in sensing duration, delay and energy consumption. Cluster based spectrum sensing provides similar sensing performance with reduced computational cost [15].

In this paper, an energy detector based cooperative spectrum sensing is proposed using Fuzzy c-means clustering. The problem has been identified as a multi-clustering problem where the objective is to organize the received PU energy values in multiple fuzzy classes or partitions. At the initial step, multiple cooperating SUs measure the energy content of the received PU signal separately and send it to the cognitive base station (CBS). CBS uses a selection combiner to accept the strongest energy content. FCM algorithm is now utilized to categorize the best energy values for different channel conditions in four fuzzy classes. Finally the sensing metrics, i.e. probability of detection and the probability of false alarm are measured to identify the effectiveness of the proposed approach.

The remainder of the paper is organized as follows. The system model is presented in Section 2, while the proposed algorithm for cooperative spectrum sensing is discussed in Section 3. Numerical results are then demonstrated in Section 4 to highlight the efficacy of proposed approach. Finally, the paper is concluded in Section 5.

2   System Model

The proposed system is shown in Fig. 1 along with the different signals at the respective time slots. It is assumed that K number of unlicensed SUs exist in the cognitive radio network (CRN). All users take part in cooperative spectrum sensing to reliably detect the presence or absence of PU. As shown in Fig. 2 the sensing interval T_s is divided into several slots with the duration of each slot being t_s. Each of these slots is further divided into two sub-slots, t_{s1} and t_{s2}. Each SU calculates the received PU signal energy during first sensing sub-slot t_{s1}. In the next sub-slot t_{s2}, all the SUs send their measured energy values

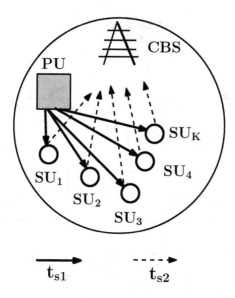

Fig. 1. System Model

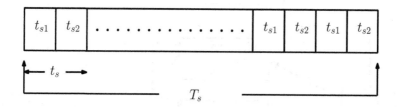

Fig. 2. Frame structure

to cognitive base station (CBS) in a common control channel using a multiple access protocol. CBS contains a selection combiner which is utilized to select the strongest PU signal energy.

The signal received by a specific SU during t_{s1} may be specified by

$$y_i(n) = \phi h_{pi} x_p(n) + v_i(n) \tag{1}$$

It is assumed that each SU observes N number of PU samples during t_{s1}. The symbol ϕ indicates the activity of PU, i.e. $\phi = 1$ indicates presence of PU signal (binary hypothesis $\mathcal{H}_1$) and $\phi = 0$ indicates no transmission from PU (binary hypothesis $\mathcal{H}_0$). The classical binary hypothesis is summarized below:

$$\mathcal{H}_1: \quad y_i(n) = h_{pi} x_p(n) + v_i(n) \tag{2}$$
$$\mathcal{H}_0: \quad y_i(n) = v_i(n) \tag{3}$$

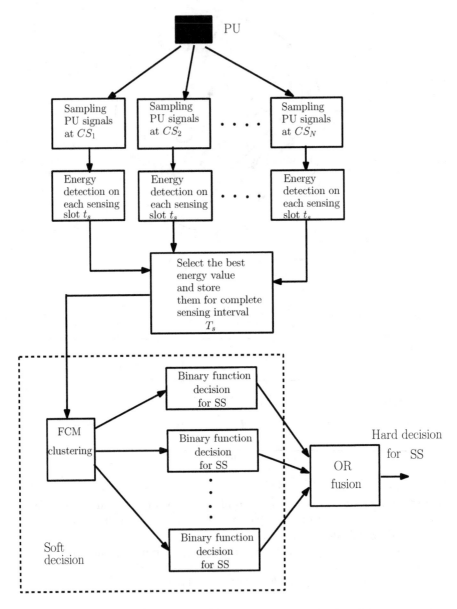

Fig. 3. Block Diagram of cooperative spectrum sensing

Primary user's signal is denoted by $x_p(n)$ which follows circularly symmetric complex Gaussian (CSCG) distribution with zero mean and variance $E[|x_p(n)|^2] = P_p$. For simplicity, it is assumed that the PU samples are mutually independent, i.e. $x_p(n) \neq x_p(m)$ for $n \neq m$. The wireless channels are modeled as flat fading channels. The symbol h_{pi} denotes flat fading coefficient of the link between PU and i^{th} SU SU_i, $\forall i = 1, ..., K$ and $h_{pi} \sim \mathcal{CN}(0, d_{pi}^{-\alpha})$. Here the distance between PU and SU_i is specified by d_{pi} and α denotes the path loss exponent. The noise $v_i(n)$ at SU_i is also modeled as independent and identically distributed (i.i.d.) CSCG noise with zero mean and variance $E[|v_i(n)|^2] = P_n$.

As shown in Fig. 3, each SU_i measures PU signal energy for SS purpose using the received PU signal $y_i(n)$. The received PU signal energy (at SU_i) is calculated as follows: $E_i = \sum_{n=1}^{N} |y_i(n)|^2$. During t_{s2}, CBS collects the measured PU signal energy values from SUs. The vector containing all the measured PU energy values at CBS from the SUs is specified by $E = \{E_i\}_{i=1}^{K}$. As already mentioned, CBS selects the strongest PU signal energy, i.e. $E_{max} = \max E$. Different values of E_{max} are calculated for different channel conditions and are stored in an 1×10000 array E'_{max}.

3   Proposed Method

This section focuses on improving the sensing reliability using FCM. As previously mentioned, E_{max} values for different channel conditions are stored in E'_{max} in CBS. However, the values of E_{max} may vary over a wide range due to the variations in propagation parameters. Therefore, different categories may exist between PU being absent $\phi = 0$ and present $\phi = 1$, and these categories can be better distinguished using FCM. To implement and verify the detector response, a binary data pattern G is produced that corresponds to $\phi = 1$ and $\phi = 0$ to generate hypothesis $\mathcal{H}_1$ and $\mathcal{H}_0$ of Eq.(2) and (3) respectively. Accordingly, PU signal energy is calculated at different SUs. Received PU signal energy stored in E'_{max} are categorized into four different classes; PU strongly present, PU moderately present, PU weakly present, PU absent. The steps of the cooperative spectrum sensing considered here are shown in Fig. 3.

3.1   Fuzzy C-Means Algorithm

FCM [2] is a classical clustering algorithm extensively used in Pattern Recognition problems. FCM is utilized to classify a specific set of P dimensional data points $\mathbf{Y} = [Y_1, Y_2, ..., Y_n]$ into a set of c fuzzy classes or partitions A_i. The steps of FCM algorithm are specified in details in Algorithm 1. Two specific conditions satisfied by the algorithm are as follows:

1. The sum of membership values of any component of $\mathbf{Y}$ (e.g. Y_j) in all c fuzzy classes is 1.

$$\sum_{i=1}^{c} \mu_{A_i}(Y_j) = 1 \quad \forall \ j = 1, ...n \tag{4}$$

where $\mu_{A_i}(Y_j)$ is the membership value of Y_j.

2. All the data points must not belong to the same class with membership 1.

$$0 < \sum_{j=1}^{n} \mu_{A_i}(Y_j) < n \quad \forall \ i = 1, ...c \tag{5}$$

Algorithm 1: Fuzzy c-means Clustering Algorithm

Input : Initial membership values $\mu_{A_i}(Y_j)$ $\forall$ $i = 1, ...c$
  $\forall$ $j = 1, ...n$
Output: Final Cluster Centers.
begin
  while $|CURRENT\mu_{A_i}(Y_j) - OLD\mu_{A_i}(Y_j)| \leq \epsilon = 0.0001(say)$ **do**
    for $i = 1$ *to* c **do**
      Find the value of V_i using the equation
      $$V_i = \frac{\sum_{j=1}^{n}(\mu_{A_i}(Y_j))^m Y_j}{\sum_{j=1}^{n}(\mu_{A_i}(Y_j))^m} \quad for \ \ m > 1$$
    end
    for $j = 1$ *to* n **do**
      for $i = 1$ *to* c **do**
        Call $\mu_{A_i}(Y_j)$ as OLD$\mu_{A_i}(Y_j)$
        if $||Y_j - V_i||^2 > 0$ **then**
          evaluate $\mu_{A_i}(Y_j)$ using the equation
          $$\mu_{A_i}(Y_j) = \left[\sum_{k=1}^{c}\left(\frac{||Y_j - V_i||^2}{||Y_j - V_k||^2}\right)^{\frac{1}{(m-1)}}\right]^{-1}$$
          Call it CURRENT$\mu_{A_i}(Y_j)$
        else
          1. Set $\mu_{A_i}(Y_j) = 1$, call it CURRENT$\mu_{A_i}(Y_j)$
          2. Set $\mu_{A_k}(Y_j) = 1$, for $k \neq i$
          call it CURRENT$\mu_{A_k}(Y_j)$
        end
      end
    end
  end
end

The cluster centers (V_i) of the given c classes and their membership values (μ_{A_i}) are related by the following expression

$$V_i = \frac{\sum_{j=1}^{n}(\mu_{A_i}(Y_j))^m Y_j}{\sum_{j=1}^{n}(\mu_{A_i}(Y_j))^m} \tag{6}$$

Here $m(m > 1)$ is any real number that influences the membership grade.

$$\mu_{A_i}(Y_j) = \left[\sum_{k=1}^{c}\left(\frac{||Y_j - V_i||^2}{||Y_j - V_k||^2}\right)^{\frac{1}{(m-1)}}\right]^{-1} \tag{7}$$

Therefore, the cluster centers of four different clusters are calculated using FCM. Here four classes indicate strong presence, moderate presence, weak presence and absence of PU signal. Now, each measured energy value stored in E'_{max}

can be placed under one of these four classes by comparing them with the cluster centers. At first, $d_i = |V_i - E_{max}| \ \forall i = 1,....4$ are calculated for a specific energy value. The objective is to find i^* s.t. $d_{i^*} = min\{d_1, d_2, d_3, d_4\}$. Based on the value of i^*, the specific energy value is classified in one of the four classes (identified by binary functions c_1, c_2, c_3, c_4). Here, $c_1 =$ PU strongly present, $c_2 =$ PU moderately present, $c_3 =$ PU weakly present, $c_4 =$ PU absent.

$$c_1 = \begin{cases} 1 & i^* = 1 \\ 0 & otherwise \end{cases}$$

$$c_2 = \begin{cases} 1 & i^* = 2 \\ 0 & otherwise \end{cases}$$

$$c_3 = \begin{cases} 1 & i^* = 3 \\ 0 & otherwise \end{cases}$$

$$c_4 = \begin{cases} 1 & i^* = 4 \\ 0 & otherwise \end{cases}$$

Now, the results from c_1, c_2 and c_3 are logically OR-ed to form the resultant binary decision function C. The binary data pattern G and C are then used to calculate P_{det} and P_f depending on the hypothesis $\mathcal{H}_1$ and $\mathcal{H}_0$, respectively.

The performance of the proposed algorithm is measured by three metrics, probability of detection, probability of false alarm, detection accuracy (AUC).
(1) Probability of detection (P_{det}) is defined as the fraction of the instances correctly detecting PU's presence (placed in classes PU strongly present, PU present, PU rarely present).
(2) Probability of false alarm (P_f) is defined as the fraction of the instances erroneously detecting PU's presence in PU absent scenario.
(3) Detection accuracy (ACC) is defined as the ratio of the total number of correctly detected PU status (i.e. individual status of PU present and absent are correctly identified) to the total number of PU status considered in simulation i.e. the length of binary pattern G.

4   Numerical Results

This section presents the numerical results to evaluate the performance of the proposed approach. To improve the sensing reliability over multipath radio mobile channel, Monte Carlo Simulations are done. 10000 Monte Carlo simulations are performed to identify and store the best PU signal energy values during 10000 sensing slots t_s taking into account the variability in sensing channels. The distances from the PU to the SUs are assumed to be significantly large compared to the distances between the SUs, i.e. $d_{pi} = d_{pc}$. Let, $\mathcal{P}(\mathcal{H}_1)$ and $\mathcal{P}(\mathcal{H}_0)$ represent the probabilities that PU is present and absent respectively, i.e. $\mathcal{P}(\mathcal{H}_0) = \mathcal{P}(\phi = 0)$ and $\mathcal{P}(\mathcal{H}_1) = \mathcal{P}(\phi = 1)$. The set of simulation parameters are as follows: $P_n = 0$ dBW, $d_{pc} = 1$ m, $\alpha = 4$, $\mathcal{P}(\mathcal{H}_0) = 0.70$ and $\mathcal{P}(\mathcal{H}_1) = 0.30$. Sampling rate of energy detection is specified at $f_s = 6$ MHz.

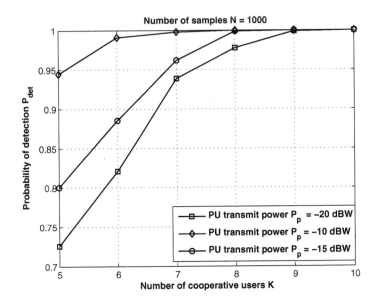

Fig. 4. Probability of detection P_{det} vs. Number of cooperative users K

Table 1. Detection Accuracy (ACC)

Conventional energy detector $P_p = -20$ dB	Proposed approach $P_p = -20$ dB	Conventional energy detector $P_p = -15$ dB	Proposed approach $P_p = -15$ dB
0.61	0.85	0.81	0.92

Fig. 4 shows the variation of detection probability P_{det} with the increasing number of cooperative users K. In this case, the number of samples N for the received PU signal is set at 1000. As $f_s = 6$ MHz, the required sensing time $t_s = 0.16$ ms, which is realistic. From the figure it is observed that P_{det} increases with the increase in diversity, i.e. increase in K. P_{det} value increases from 0.73 to 1 as K value is increased from 5 to 10 when P_p is fixed at -20 dBW. Furthermore, with an increase in P_p, PU SNR increases resulting in the improvement in P_{det} value. Approximately 10% and 30% increase in P_{det} value is noted for 5 and 10 dBW increase in P_p value, respectively when K value is set at 5.

The variation of P_{det} with the number of received PU signal samples N is shown in Fig. 5 where the value of K is set to 6. From the figure it can inferred that detection probability, i.e. P_{det} increases with increase in N value. When P_P is set at -6 dBW, about 29% increase in P_{det} value is noted as the N value is increased from 500 to 1500. Similar to Fig. 4, P_{det} improves with the increase in PU SNR. An increment of 16% in P_{det} value is observed for 4 dBW increase in P_p value when N value is set at 500.

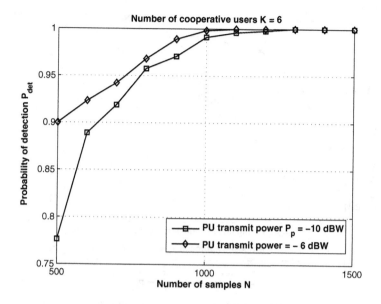

Fig. 5. Probability of detection P_{det} vs. Number of samples N

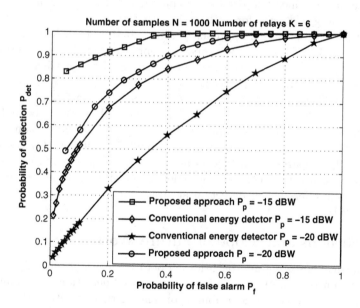

Fig. 6. Receiver operating characteristic curves (P_{det} vs. P_f)

Fig. 6 illustrates the receiver operating characteristics (ROC) curve which plots P_{det} against P_f. In this case, the values of N and K are fixed at 1000 and 6, respectively. The ROC curve indicates that an increase in P_{det} value with

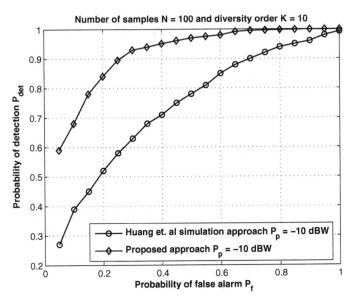

Fig. 7. Comparison of receiver operating characteristic curve (P_{det} vs. P_f) with [7]

the increase in P_f value. The results are compared with the performance of a conventional energy detector for both $P_p = -15$ dBW and $P_p = -20$ dBW. It is observed that the proposed approach performs better than the conventional energy detector. For $P_f = 0.4$, the proposed approach provides about 60% and 17% higher P_{det} compared to the conventional energy detector when $P_p = -20$ dBW and $P_p = -15$ dBW, respectively.

In Fig. 7, ROC characteristic (P_{det} vs. P_f) is compared with [7]. In this case, the simulation parameters are set as follows: $P_p = -10$ dBW, $N = 100$ and $K = 10$. It can be observed that the proposed approach performs better than [7]. For $P_f = 0.10$, the proposed approach provides about 74% higher P_{det} compared to [7]. Table 1 compares the detection accuracy of the proposed system with the detection accuracy of conventional energy detector. It is noted that the proposed system offers better detection accuracy for $P_p = -20$ dB and $P_p = -15$ dB, respectively.

5   Conclusions and Scope of Future Work

Fuzzy C-Means Clustering approach for cooperative spectral sensing based on energy detection is performed in this work. Improved detection performance in binary hypothesis problem of SS is found considering this a multiple (four) class problem where energy values calculated at different SUs are clustered as an indicator of strong, moderate, weakly presence and absence of PU. Extensive simulation results are shown to highlight high P_{det} value (above ~ 0.9) at very low SNR values (-10 to -20 dBW). Simulation results for SS performance simultaneously show high P_{det} value at low P_f values through ROC and performance result is shown to be significantly high compared to the existing works.

The present work may be extended as compressed sensing based cooperative SS to accomplish an energy efficient algorithm.

References

1. Akyildiz, I.F., Lo, B.F., Balakrishnan, R.: Cooperative spectrum sensing in cognitive radio networks: A survey. Phys. Commun. 4(1), 40–62 (2011)
2. Bezdek, J.C.: Pattern Recognition with Fuzzy Objective Function Algorithms. Plenum Press, New York (1981)
3. Federal Communications Commission Spectrum Policy Task Force, Rep. ET Docket no. 02-135 (November 2002)
4. Fanzi, Z., Li, C., Tian, Z.: Distributed compressive spectrum sensing in cooperative multihop cognitive networks. IEEE Journal of Selected Topics in Signal Processing 5(1), 37–48 (2011)
5. Ghozzi, M., Marx, F., Dohler, M., Palicot, J.: Cyclostatilonarilty-based test for detection of vacant frequency bands. In: 1st International Conference on Cognitive Radio Oriented Wireless Networks and Communications, pp. 1–5 (June 2006)
6. Haykin, S.: Cognitive radio: brain-empowered wireless communications. IEEE Journal on Selected Areas in Commun 23(2), 201–220 (2005)
7. Huang, S., Chen, H., Zhang, Y., Zhao, F.: Energy-efficient cooperative spectrum sensing with amplify-and-forward relaying. IEEE Commun. Lett. 16(4), 450–453 (2012)
8. Lim, T.J., Zhang, R., Liang, Y.C., Zeng, Y.: GLRT-based spectrum sensing for cognitive radio. In: IEEE Global Telecommunications Conference, pp. 1–5 (2008)
9. Lopez-Benitez, M., Casadevall, F.: Improved energy detection spectrum sensing for cognitive radio. IET Communications 6(8), 785–796 (2012)
10. Mishra, S., Sahai, A., Brodersen, R.: Cooperative sensing among cognitive radios. In: IEEE International Conference on Communications, ICC, vol. 4, pp. 1658–1663 (June 2006)
11. Mohammadi, A., Taban, M.R., Abouei, J., Torabi, H.: Fuzzy likelihood ratio test for cooperative spectrum sensing in cognitive radio. Signal Processing 93(5), 1118–1125 (2013)
12. OFCOM: Digital Dividend Review, A statement on our approach towards awarding the digital dividend (December 2007)
13. Tandra, R., Sahai, A.: Fundamental limits on detection in low snr under noise uncertainty. In: International Conference on Wireless Networks, Communications and Mobile Computing, vol. 1 (June 2005)
14. Tian, Z., Giannakis, G.: A wavelet approach to wideband spectrum sensing for cognitive radios. In: 1st International Conference on Cognitive Radio Oriented Wireless Networks and Communications, pp. 1–5 (June 2006)
15. Wang, L., Wang, J., Ding, G., Song, F., Wu, Q.: A survey of cluster-based cooperative spectrum sensing in cognitive radio networks. In: Cross Strait Quad-Regional Radio Science and Wireless Technology Conference (CSQRWC), vol. 1, pp. 247–251 (July 2011)
16. Yang, W., Cai, Y., Xu, Y.: A fuzzy collaborative spectrum sensing scheme in cognitive radio. In: International Symposium on Intelligent Signal Processing and Communication Systems, pp. 566–569 (November 2007)
17. Yucek, T., Arslan, H.: A survey of spectrum sensing algorithms for cognitive radio applications. IEEE Commun. Surveys Tutorials 11(1), 116–130 (2009)
18. Zhang, H., Wang, X.: A fuzzy decision scheme for cooperative spectrum sensing in cognitive radio. In: IEEE 73rd Vehicular Technology Conference (VTC Spring), pp. 1–4 (May 2011)

A Fast Method for Network Topology Generating

Vladimir Shakhov, Olga Sokolova, and Anastasia Yurgenson

Institute of Computational Mathematics and Mathematical Geophysics SB RAS
Prospect Akademika Lavrentjeva 6, 630090 Novosibirsk, Russia
{shakhov,olga,nastya}@rav.sscc.ru
http://www.sscc.ru/

Abstract. Authors provide a new method that can speedup simulation of wireless sensor networks or ad hoc networks. Performance improvement has been achieved by fast generating of pseudo-random UDG graphs with prescribed properties. Numerical results demonstrate that the proposed method achieves an essential computational cost reduction in comparison with the standard approach.

Keywords: wireless sensor networks, pseudo-random graph generator, UDG graphs.

1 Introduction

Simulation technique is the primary methodological framework for research and development of communication networks. For this purpose, an analytical approach based on queue theory or graph theory has been often used as well. However, its use requires quit simplifying assumptions since more realistic assumptions make comprehensive analysis extremely difficult. The main disadvantages of empirical methods include inability to test network sensitivity and tune performance. Thus, simulation technique is an indispensable tool for the research and development of wireless sensor networks (WSNs). It allows to get significant comparative studies of various MAC protocols, traffic-aggregation schemes, energy efficient routing algorithms, and hence, a researcher can determinate which protocol performs better from the quality-of-service point of view in a concrete situation.

One of the most important things of WSNs simulation is the pseudo-random graphs generator. A researcher has to describe the structure of links connecting pairs of sensors. For these purposes, pseudo-random graphs are generally used. A network topology strongly influences the choice and performance of protocols. For example, the network latencies and collisions rate in some MAC protocols are determined by data gathering tree properties [1]. Therefore, it is very important to consider the nature and mechanism of network topology generating, and the manner in which it depends on the features of the wireless sensor network.

There are a large number of studies in the area of networks simulation, but there is a lack of comprehensive evaluation of existing methods for WSNs topology generation. In most investigations of wireless networks, when topology-based

M. Jonsson et al. (Eds.): MACOM 2014, LNCS 8715, pp. 96–101, 2014.

algorithms are evaluated, a unit disk graph (UDG or UDG-graph) is generally used in assumptions of the simulation framework. A description of common simulated scenario contains a square area in which sensors are uniformly distributed, the side of the square and the sensor coverage (transmission) radius. At the same time, the network connectivity property has to be supported. However, the corresponding method is not described. It is hard (sometimes impossible) to provide a reliable performance comparison of alternative WSNs protocols due to the absence of unified network topology generating approach. To fill this gap we provide an algorithm for WSNs topology generation and discuss the related problems.

The rest of the paper is organized as follows. Section 2 reviews some necessary background material. It includes properties of communication system topology and the concept of a unit disk graph. Related works are discussed. Section 3 describes the proposed method. Performance analysis is discussed in Section 4. Finally, we conclude the paper in Section 5.

2 Preliminaries

The process of research and development of WSNs protocols requires adequate models for network topology. Given a set of sensor nodes, distributed in some area, it is necessary to specify which nodes are able to receive a data from other nodes. The network topology has been described by a graph $G = (V, E)$, where the set V consists of vertices (sensor nodes) and the set E (edges) describes the adjacency relation between nodes. The most popular model for sensor networks structures is the so-called Unit Disk Graph. Let us provide the formal definition of UDG-graph from the textbooks [2], [3].

Definition: A graph $G = (V, E)$ is UDG-graph if any two nodes are adjacent if and only if their Euclidean distance is at most 1 (or other positive constant). That is, for arbitrary $u, v \in V$, it holds that $\{u, v\} \in E \Leftrightarrow |u, v| \leq 1$.

In literature it has been mentioned that UDG-graphs adequately describes a networks structure (see, for example [5]). At present it becomes the standard way for performance analysis of ad hoc and wireless sensor networks. UDG represents an idealized sensor network with multiple nodes. Network nodes are arranged in a Euclidean plane, and it is assumed the nodes have got equal radius for data transmission. They can transmit packets to each other, if they are within each other's signal reachability. The deployment phase in WSNs simulation is critical and requires careful organization.

Taking into account characteristics of real networks, a reliable generator has to deliver UDG graphs with some additional properties, for example, graph connectivity, the limitations for graph diameter, desired nodes density etc. The common used approach of UDG graphs generating is as follows. WSNs nodes are distributed uniformly, randomly and independently from each other in some area [7]. Next, for each pair of nodes the edge presence is computed. If the generated graph is not connected then one is rejected. Depending on desired properties of UDG graph, some additional actions can be made. It can be a hard time-consuming operation. Let us introduce the term "Traditional" for this method.

There are some other approaches for WSNs topology generating. In [6] authors propose a generator for sensor network, which is able to generate topologies of wireless sensor networks and, additionally, provides important characteristics of sensor nodes, such as energy parameters. Authors offer to use a deterministic regular structure (grid) for network topology. It is generally unrealistic scenario. However, this approach can be applied in some special cases.

In article [8] authors present algorithms (for example C-CRUGs) for generating connected graphs. The main idea is as follows. The next generated vertex is added to the vertex with minimum degree. The method provides network connectivity. However, it often creates graphs with locally vertices crowding (see Fig. 1a). Therefore, if full coverage of WSNs deployment area is required (see Fig. 1b), then the method is not convenient.

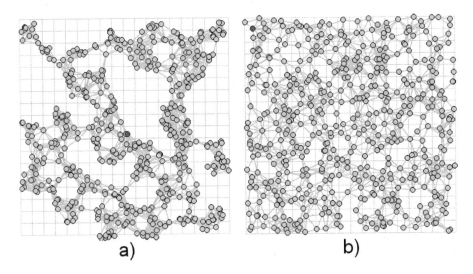

Fig. 1. The graphs are generated by the algorithm [8] and "Traditional" algorithm

Taking into account WSNs properties, we formulate the criteria for efficient generator. First, pseudo-random UDG-graph has to be connected. Second, it provides full coverage of WSNs deployment area. And next, the computational time is reasonable. In next section we describe a new method that can speedup simulation of wireless sensor networks or ad hoc networks. Performance improvement has been achieved by generating pseudo-random UDG graphs with prescribed properties. Numerical results demonstrate that the proposed method achieves an essential computational cost reduction in comparison with the "traditional" approach.

3   Proposed Algorithm

We construct an auxiliary grid with some step L_{step} for given square area (the side equals A), where the grid step $L_{step} = R/\sqrt{5}$. Here, R is a sensing (and transmission) range. Thus, the WSNs deployment area is divided into $l \times l$ cells, where $l = A/L_{step}$. Not reduce generality, we assume that l is an integer value. Any vertex in a cell covers this cell. Any two nodes from adjacent cells are connected. Every grid's cell should contain at least one node. The main idea of our algorithm is as follows. At first, we place one vertex in every cell uniformly (to fulfill the coverage condition), then we choose a cell $L_{i,j}$ and put a random number of nodes to this cell. This number has got the Poisson distribution. Here, the following property is used. If vertices are uniformly distributed in some area then number of vertices in subarea can be approximated by the Poisson distribution [9].

All new added nodes are obviously connected. For a new vertex we check edge presence only in the set of some neighbor cells $\Omega_{i,j} = \{L[i + m, j + k] \mid m, k \in \{0; \pm 1; \pm 2; \pm 3\}, 1 < |m| + |k| \leq 4\}$. This approach decreases number of computing operations.

Algorithm 1. Grid + Poisson

---

for $i, j = 1 \ldots L_{size}$ **do**
    to generate one random vertex $v_{x,y}$ in the cell $L[i, j]$;
    to check distance in $\Omega_{i,j}$
end for
$n_{curr} = n - L_{size}^2$; – the number of non-generating vertices
for $i, j = 1 \ldots L_{size}$ **do**
    $s_{i,j} = Poisson(\lambda) > 0$ – the number of vertices in cell $L[i, j]$
    to generate $(s_{i,j} - 1)$ vertices in the cell $L[i, j]$;
    to check distance in $\Omega_{i,j}$;
    $n_{curr} = n_{curr} - (s_{i,j} - 1)$; To decrease $s_{i,j}$ in previous line if $n_{curr} < 0$
    if $n_{curr} = 0$ **then** break loops;
end for

---

4   Performance Comparison

Let us describe the simulation environment. The considered area is a square 17x17 cells, $R = 30$.

On the Fig.2 and Fig.3 we present distributions of nodes-per-cell and vertices degrees. It is based on the average for hundred pseudo-random graphs.

The properties of graphs generated by novel and common used algorithms are very closed. However, the novel algorithm is twice faster. Remark, here we do not use the procedure of coverage control for "Traditional" method. Otherwise, the performance of proposed algorithm becomes better still.

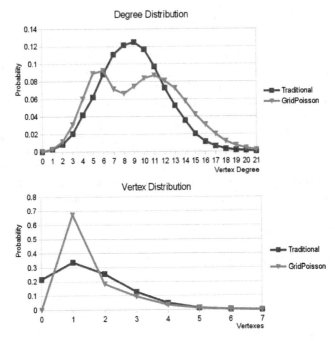

Fig. 2. Degree and vertices distribution. $|V| = 500$.

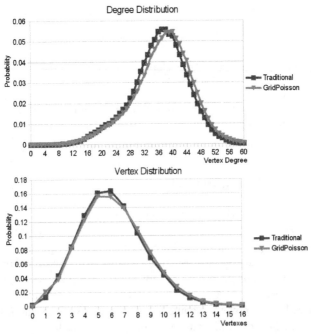

Fig. 3. Degree and vertices distribution. $|V| = 2000$.

5   Conclusion

We provide a new method that can speedup simulation of wireless sensor networks, ad hoc networks, cognitive radio network etc. Performance improvement is achieved by generating pseudo-random UDG graphs with prescribed properties. Thus, additional treatment of the generated graphs is not required and the graph rejection procedure is not used. Numerical results demonstrate that the proposed method achieves an essential computational cost reduction in comparison with the standard approach.

Acknowledgments. This research was supported by grants of the Russian Foundation for Basic Research under Grants 14-07-00769.

References

1. Lu, G., Krishnamachari, B., Raghavendra, C.S.: An adaptive energy efficient and low-latency MAC for data gathering in wireless sensor networks. In: Proceedings of 18th International Parallel and Distributed Processing Symposium, April 26-30, p. 224 (2004)
2. Boukerche, A.: Algorithms and Protocols for Wireless Sensor Networks. John Wiley & Sons Inc. (2008)
3. Clark, B.N., Colbourn, C.J., Johnson, D.S.: Unit disk graphs. Discrete Mathematics 86(13), 165–177 (1990)
4. Wagner, D., Wattenhofer, R. (eds.): Algorithms for Sensor and Ad Hoc Networks. LNCS, vol. 4621. Springer, Heidelberg (2007)
5. Dong, D., Liao, X., Liu, Y., Li, X., Pang, Z.: Fine-Grained Location-Free Planarization in Wireless Sensor Networks. IEEE Transactions on Mobile Computing 12(5), 971–983 (2013)
6. Camilo, T., Silva, J.S., Rodrigues, A., Boavida, F.: GENSEN: A topology generator for real wireless sensor networks deployment. In: Obermaisser, R., Nah, Y., Puschner, P., Rammig, F.J. (eds.) SEUS 2007. LNCS, vol. 4761, pp. 436–445. Springer, Heidelberg (2007)
7. Seo, J., Kim, M., Hur, I., Choi, W., Choo, H.: DRDT: Distributed and Reliable Data Transmission with Cooperative Nodes for LossyWireless Sensor Networks. Sensors 10(4), 2793–2811 (2010)
8. Onat, F.A., Stojmenovic, I., Yanikomeroglu, H.: Generating random graphs for the simulation of wireless ad hoc, actuator, sensor, and internet networks. Pervasive and Mobile Computing 4, 597–615 (2008)
9. Song, L.: Random graph models for wireless communication networks. PhD Thesis, https://qmro.qmul.ac.uk/jspui/handle/123456789/426

Self-similar Nature of 3D Video Formats

Amela Zeković[1,2] and Irini Reljin[1]

[1] University of Belgrade, School of Electrical Engineering, Serbia
amelaz@viser.edu.rs,
http://www.etf.bg.ac.rs/
[2] School of Electrical and Computer Engineering of Applied Studies,
Belgrade, Serbia

Abstract. Communication network traffic shows self-similar behavior with long-range dependency (LRD). We analyzed self-similar nature of different 3D video formats, namely the multiview (MV) video, the frame sequential (FS) and the side-by-side (SBS) representation video formats using the visual and more rigorous methods. Analyses were performed by the aggregated variance method, the R/S statistics method, and the multifractal based multiscale method. We used publicly available long full HD video frame-size traces of 3D videos. Additionally, self-similarity of 3D videos with streaming approach with aggregation of frames is showed.

Keywords: 3D video, burstiness, Hurst parameter, self-similarity.

1 Introduction

Three-dimensional (3D) videos are becoming increasingly present in wireland and wireless networks, and due to the high data content they present significant load in the network [7,11,15,19]. This impact of 3D video on network traffic causes a need of improving means to handle this type of data.

Previous studies of 3D video are related to 3D video coding techniques and their improvement [4,13], design and physical realization of system chain for production, transport, and display of this video type [21,22], as well as the effective ways of modeling of the 3D video transport [5].

One line of research of image and video follows presence of fractal properties [14], especially self-similarity in this type of data, for example self-similarity in images used in fractal compression, [10].

In [18] it was shown that communication network traffic has self-similar behavior and even exhibits changes in delay in losses as a consequence. Also, it was shown that self-similar long-range dependent behavior is the reason behind appearance of bursty traffic which exceeds average traffic levels [9,16].

Quantity of data of 3D video and its growing presence in the network traffic motivates thorough understanding of this video type. We examined self-similarity of 3D video representation formats: the multiview (MV), the frame sequential (FS), and the frame compatible (FS) side-by-side (SBS) representation formats. Used graphical and more rigorous statistical methods showed self-similar behavior of 3D video in the long-range dependency area. In the analyses, we used

M. Jonsson et al. (Eds.): MACOM 2014, LNCS 8715, pp. 102–111, 2014.

publicly available long frame-size traces of 3D video, [17,1]. These results can further be used for effective modeling of 3D video, having in mind its self-similar nature,[18,2].

The paper is structured in four sections. Section 2 gives short review of definition and estimation methods for self-similarity. Section 3 contains description of used 3D video representation formats data and results of performed analyses. In Sect. 4 some final remarks are presented.

2 Definition and Estimation of Self-similarity

The real-valued process $X(t)$, $t \in \mathbb{R}$, is self-similar with the parameter H if, for any positive factor c, finite-dimensional distributions for $X(ct)$, $t \in \mathbb{R}$, are equal in distributions to $c^H X(t)$, $t \in \mathbb{R}$, [14,3,18]. Thus, typical sample paths of self-similar process look qualitatively the same, irrespective of the time scale in which are considered. This does not mean that the same picture repeats exactly, it is rather the general impression that remains the same.

One of the advantages of using self-similar model of time series is that the degree of self-similarity is expressed using only single number, parameter H. This parameter is sometimes called the Hurst exponent, after Herold Hurst, who did early work in scaling river fluctuations.

Values of the Hurst parameter can be divided in three distinctive categories: $0 < H < 1/2$ that characterize short-range dependent (SRD) processes, $H = 1/2$ for random walk processes, and $1/2 < H < 1$ that is characteristic of long-range dependent (LRD) processes. The case $H = 1/2$ characterizes processes with independent increments, i.e. $X(t_2) - X(t_1)$ and $X(t_3) - X(t_2)$ with $t_1 < t_2 < t_3$ being independent in the sense of probability theory, their correlation is zero. Parameter H in the range $0 < H < 1/2$ characterize processes with negative correlation increments, while values in the range $1/2 < H < 1$ are characteristic of process with positive correlation between increments, i.e. if the graph of X tends to increase for some t_0, then it tends to continue to increase for $t > t_0$, [14].

It is shown that network traffic exhibits self-similarity, and as a measure of the degree of self-similarity the Hurst parameter can be used. This parameter shows level of burstiness in traffic, where higher values indicate higher burstiness in traffic, [9,16].

In this paper, we used three methods to test for self-similarity in 3D videos. Used algorithms are described shortly, while detailed descriptions of the methods can be found in [3,18,9,6]. We used Aggregated variance method, R/S statistics method, and a method based on correlation between multifractal analysis and Hurst parameter, i.e. multiscale method. Used algorithms are successfully tested using fractional Gaussian noise process with a specified value of the Hurst parameter,[20].

We examined 3D video formats using frame-size traces. Let N denote the number of frames in a trace, X_n, $n = 1,\ldots,N$, denote the frame size, $\overline{X}$

sample mean, and S_X^2 denote sample variance. The aggregated frame size traces, with aggregation level a, are defined as

$$X_n^{(a)} = \frac{1}{a} \sum_{j=(n-1)a+1}^{na} X_j, \; n = 1, 2, \ldots, N/a \qquad (1)$$

i.e. the aggregated frame size trace is formed by averaging original frame size trace over non-overlapping boxes of size a. Variance of the aggregated trace is now

$$S_X^{2\,(a)} = \frac{1}{N/a} \sum_{n=1}^{N/a} (X_n^{(a)} - \overline{X})^2. \qquad (2)$$

This procedure is repeated for different values of the aggregation level, a. We used the aggregation levels that are multiplies of the group of picture (GoP) size to avoid intra-GoP correlations. Values of aggregation level and variance of the aggregated trace are plotted on the log-log plot. Resulting point should plot straight line with slope $\beta = 2H - 2$. For estimation of the slope, we used the linear least squares fit. If X has short-range or no dependence, the obtained slope should be equal to -1.

The second method for Hurst parameter estimation, that we used, is R/S statistics method. The series X_n is subdivided in K non-overlapping blocks. Now, the rescaled adjusted range $R(t_i, d)/S(t_i, d)$ are computed for a number of values d, where $t_i = N/K(i-1)+1$ are starting points of the blocks which satisfy $(t_i - 1) + d \le N$,

$$R(t_i, d) = \max\{0, W(t_i, 1), \ldots, W(t_1, d)\} - \min\{0, W(t_i, 1), \ldots, W(t_1, d)\} \qquad (3)$$

where,

$$W(t_i, k) = \sum_{j=1}^{k} X_{t_i+j-1} - k\left(\frac{1}{d}\sum_{j=1}^{d} X_{t_i+j-1}\right), \; k = 1, \ldots, d \qquad (4)$$

and $S^2(t_i, d)$ denotes sample variance of $X_{t_i}, \ldots, X_{t_i+d-1}$. For each value of d number of R/S samples is obtained. This number decreases for larger values of d because of the limiting conditions for t_i values. Plotting $\log(R(t_i, d)/S(t_i, d))$ versus $\log d$ results in R/S plot, also known as pox plot. The slope of the regression line of R/S samples is an estimate of the Hurst parameter.

The first step in evaluating the Hurst parameter by the multiscale method is covering the self-similar series with non-overlapping boxes of size ϵ_k, as in the multifractal analysis by the method of moments. Now, partition functions, defined as

$$X_q(\epsilon) = \sum \mu(\epsilon)^q \qquad (5)$$

are calculated, where q is the moment order $q \in \mathbb{R}$, and $\mu(\epsilon)$ is total value of data in the boxes of size ϵ. Function $\tau(q)$ is estimated as slopes of plots $\log(X_q(\epsilon))$ versus $\log(\epsilon)$. Approximate value of the Hurst index is now evaluated as

$$H = \frac{\tau(2) + 1}{2}. \qquad (6)$$

3   Examining 3D Video Formats Self-similarity

3.1   3D Video Data Series

In this paper, we examined three main 3D video representation formats, [15,11,8,12]. Self-similar nature of the multiview (MV), the frame sequential (FS) and the side-by-side (SBS) representation formats are examined.

The multiview (MV) contains several views of the same scene, where each view v, $v = 1, \ldots, V$, is once frame sequence in full HD 1920×1080 pixels resolution. The MV video format has the full resolution as underlaying spatial format, and frame rate f for each view v is the same as the underlaying temporal format. For coding the multiview representation format, multiview coding (MVC) is used. This type of coding, in addition to temporal and spatial redundancy, utilize inter-view redundancy. Thus, ITU reference software, referred to as JMVC, first encodes frames of the left view and then uses these frames as reference frames for encoding frames of the right view. Coding of the used MV video series is performed by reference software JMVC version 8.3.1.

The frame sequential (FS) video format has only one frame sequence, where frames from different views are interleaved. The spatial resolution of the FS format is the same as in the underlaying spatial format, while frame rate of the FS format is Vf, where V is the number of views, and f is the frame rate of the underlaying temporal format. Coding of FS video format is done by conventional single-view video encoder, and coding of used FS video series is performed by H.264 reference software JSVM version 9.19.10 in single layer encoding mode.

Frame compatible (FC) formats allow utilization of existing infrastructure and equipment for transmission and services for 3D video. These formats have one video sequence with frame rate f that is the same as in the underlaying temporal format, while having lower spatial resolution than the underlaying spatial format. For example, for the most widely used FC format, the side-by-side (SBS) format, frames are spatially sub-sampled in horizontal direction. As in the case of FS format, SBS representation also uses conventional single-view video encoder for coding, namely H.264 reference software JSVM version 9.19.10 in single layer encoding mode was used.

We performed self-similarity analysis of the multiview (MV), the frame sequential (FS), and side-by-side (SBS) 3D video representation formats using long, publicly available video frame size traces. Examined video had two views ($V = 2$), the left view and the right view, where each view had 51200 full HD 1920×1080 pixel frames, and the frame rate $f = 24$ frames/s. We performed evaluations with Tim Burton's 3D movie *Alice in Wonderland*, which is combination of a live action and computer-animated movie. We analyzed different 3D representation format of this movie, and videos with different quantization parameter settings ($q_p = 24$, $q_p = 28$, and $q_p = 34$). Group of picture (GoP) length for MV and SBS format was 16 frames, while FS format had GoP with

32 frames, to ensure that all encodings have the same playback time between intracoded (I) frames. GoP pattern was B1, which means one bi-directional (B) frame between successive intracoded (I) and predictive encoded (P) frames.

In addition to examining self-similar nature of MV, FS, and SBS 3D video format, we extended our research to self-similarity analysis of 3D video with different streaming approaches. Frames can be streamed in original one-by-one form in the case of single-view video, or each view individually for the multiview video. For the used multiview video (MV), that has two views, the left view (LV) and the right view (RV), this means that the views are streamed individually as separate video sequences. Second streaming option is to perform some kind of merging of views, such as sequential (S) merging or aggregation (combining, C). With sequential merging, frames from different views are used to form one sequence in the following order: first view 1 of frame 1, followed by view 2 of frame 1,..., followed by view V of frame 1, followed by view 1 of frame 2 ...With aggregation streaming approach, multiview frames are formed, where one multiview frame is the sum of all frames with the same frame number from different views. This approach we applied on the aggregation level of two frames (we labeled these series as MV-C 2, FS-C 2, and SBS-C 2), and on the level of group of picture (these series are labeled as MV-C 16, FS-C 16, and SBS-C 16) in results.

3.2   Self-similarity of 3D Video

The multiview (MV) video frame-size trace is graphically represented in Fig.1 (a), as a relation of frame sizes and their sequence number. This video trace is also presented for two smaller ranges of the frame number in Fig.1 (b), and Fig.1 (c). Selected ranges are highlighted in Fig.1. From Fig.1 it can be seen, qualitatively, self-similar nature of the multiview 3D video.

This self-similarity test is only graphical, and statistically more rigorous methods of showing self-similar nature of 3D video formats are necessary. In our analysis we used the aggregated variance method, R/S statistics method, and multiscale method for estimation of self-similarity in 3D video. Detailed description of these methods is given in Sect. 2. Advantage of self-similar modeling of traces is existence of only one key parameter to describe sequence, the Hurst parameter.

Graphical representation of the aggregated variance method is given in Fig. 2, while graph used in R/S statistics method is depicted in Fig. 3. These are examples of graphs used in evaluation of the Hurst parameter. As a reference, in Fig. 2 line with $k = -1$ slope is depicted, while in Fig. 3 reference lines with slopes $k_1 = 1/2$ and $k_2 = 1$ are presented. The regression lines in Fig. 2 and 3 obtained by the least squares fit have slope β. In the case of aggregated variance method, the Hurst parameter is calculated as $H = \beta/2 + 1$, while for R/S statistics

Table 1. Values of the Hurst exponent for 3D video representation formats by the aggregation method, R/S statistics method, and the multiscale method

3D video	$H_{Averaged\ Variance}$	$H_{R/S}$	$H_{Multiscale}$
LV	0.9002	0.9627	0.9284
RV	0.8844	0.9774	1.0026
MV	0.9164	0.9737	0.9118
SBS	0.9034	0.9601	0.9304
FS	0.9206	0.9881	0.9567

method as $H = \beta$. Examples of H parameter estimation presented in Fig. 2 and 3 are for the multiview 3D video representation format with quantization parameter $q_p = 28$.

Complete results of the Hurst parameter estimation for the left view (LV), the right view (RV), the multiview (MV), the side-by-side (SBS), and the frame sequential (FS) formats are given in Table 1. Quantization parameter for all video formats was $q_p = 28$. Results are obtained for the aggregated variance method, R/S statistics method and the multiscale method. From Table 1 it can be seen that values of the Hurst exponent for 3D video formats have rather high values, in the range $0.88 < H < 1.00$, indicating high level long-range dependencies in the 3D videos.

Previous results apply for videos where frames are sequenced one-by-one, while Table 2 contains results for self-similarity tests for streaming of 3D video where frames are aggregated in pairs (labeled C 2) or aggregated on the group of picture level (labeled C 16). Results indicate self-similar long-range dependent behavior of aggregated 3D videos, but with general lower values of the Hurst parameter. The side-by-side format shows the lowest level of correlated variation in sequence, while the multiview and the frame sequential have close higher values.

We examined influence of aggregation with aggregation level a and averaging in the multiview video on the self-similarity of the video using R/S statistics method. Results are presented in Table 3. Also, in Table 3 results for different values of quantization parameter are indicated, for $q_p = 24$, $q_p = 28$, and $q_p = 34$. These results indicate that the Hurst parameter has the lowest values in the case of the right view, followed by the values for the left view and finally the highest values are obtained for the multiview. Next, the R/S method of determining the Hurst index shows that an increase in values of quantization parameters leads to reduction of the Hurst index in the most of the cases. Increase in aggregation with averaging of frames, as indicated in Table 3, also in general, leads to redaction in values of the Hurst parameter.

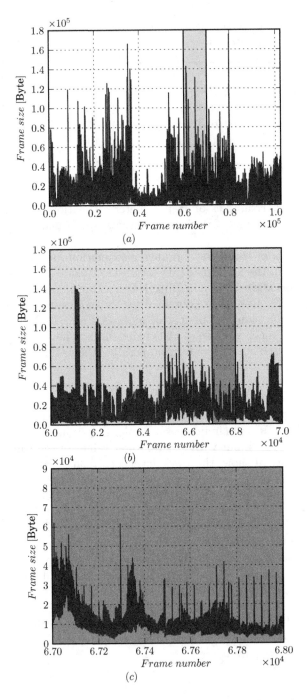

Fig. 1. Frame sizes in relation to their sequence number for the multiview 3D video: (a) whole video trace, (b) zoomed section of the video trace, and (c) further zoomed section of the video trace

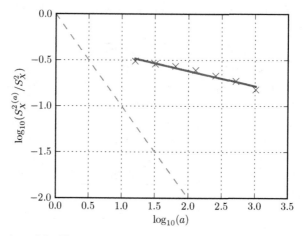

Fig. 2. Evaluation of the Hurst parameter for the multiview 3D video by the aggregated variance method

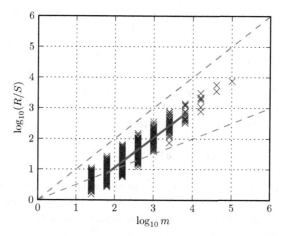

Fig. 3. Evaluation of the Hurst parameter for the multiview 3D video by R/S statistics method

Table 2. Comparison of the Hurst exponent values for 3D video formats with two aggregated frames (C 2) and GoP aggregation (C 16)

3D video	$H_{Averaged\ Variance}$	$H_{R/S}$	$H_{Multiscale}$
MV-C 2	0.8995	0.9811	0.9624
MV-C 16	0.7899	0.8681	1.0030
SBS-C 2	0.8757	0.9504	0.9819
SBS-C 16	0.5820	0.8676	1.0006
FS-C 2	0.9050	0.9860	0.9929
FS-C 16	0.8028	0.8567	1.0072

Table 3. Comparison of the values for the Hurst parameter obtained by R/S method for the multiview 3D video

a	$q_p = (24, 24, 24)$			$q_p = (28, 28, 28)$			$q_p = (34, 34, 34)$		
	LV	RV	MV	LV	RV	MV	LV	RV	MV
16	0.934	0.880	0.935	0.913	0.845	0.924	0.918	0.851	0.931
64	0.936	0.885	0.910	0.904	0.832	0.880	0.896	0.824	0.879
96	0.918	0.870	0.930	0.877	0.814	0.889	0.870	0.809	0.890
160	0.892	0.882	0.918	0.856	0.883	0.870	0.835	0.882	0.867
320	0.815	0.788	0.898	0.752	0.780	0.856	0.724	0.779	0.841
640	0.718	0.729	0.789	0.636	0.748	0.727	0.609	0.731	0.724

4   Conclusion

We analyzed 3D video representation formats: the multiview (MV), the frame sequential (FS), and the frame compatible (FC) side-by-side (SBS) formats using publicly available frame-size traces,[15,1] by the means of graphical and statistic methods: the aggregated variance method, the R/S statistics method, the multi-scale method [18,3], we showed self-similar nature of 3D video formats. Obtained values of the Hurst parameter for all examined 3D video formats fit in the area of the long-range dependency, with values around $H = 0.95$. Such high value of the Hurst parameter indicated high burstiness of the data.

Influence of streaming approach of 3D videos on the Hurst exponent values is analyzed, showing in general lower values of the parameter for streaming approach with aggregation of the frames. Effects of variation of the quantization parameter on self-similar nature of 3D video is shown for the same video with quantization parameters $q_p = 24$, $q_p = 28$, and $q_p = 34$. It is found that lower values of the Hurst parameter characterize the video with higher value of the quantization parameter, in general. It was shown that aggregation and averaging over frames also leads to lower values of the Hurst parameter.

We examined 3D video in the the multiview (MV), the frame sequential (FS), and the side-by-side (SBS) formats, where for the coding of the MV video reference software JMVC was used, while for the FS and SBS formats the reference software JSVM was selected. For future work, we plan to include examination of self-similar nature of 3D video with different coding parameters. Also, we plan to take into account influence of other 3D video parameters, such as the number of views in the video, video formats, and quantization parameters.

Our results are important for better understanding of 3D video formats in the sense that their high self-similar nature, which can further be used for more effective modeling of the videos. Variation of self-similarity of 3D videos in the case of video multiplexing will be a topic of our future research.

References

1. Video trace library, http://trace.eas.asu.edu
2. Bai, X., Shami, A.: Modeling self-similar traffic for network simulation. Technical report, NetRep-2005-01 (2005)
3. Beran, J.: Statistics for Long-Memory Processes. Chapman & Hall, New York (1994)
4. Chen, Y., Wang, Y.K., Ugur, K., Hannuksela, M.M., Lainema, J., Gabbouj, M.: The emerging MVC standard for 3D video services. EURASIP Journal on Advances in Signal Processing (2009)
5. Cosmas, J., Loo, J., Aggoun, A., Tsekleves, E.: Matlab traffic and network flow model for planning impact of 3D applications on networks. In: Proceedings of IEEE Int. Symp. on Broadband Multimedia Systems and Broadcasting (2010)
6. Crovella, M.E., Bestavros, A.: Self-similarity in World Wide Web traffic: Evidence and possible causes. IEEE/ACM Transactions on Networking 5(6), 835–846 (1997)
7. Fernando, A., Worrall, S., Ekmekcioglu, E.: 3DTV: processing and transmission of 3D video signals. John Wiley & Sons, Inc., United Kingdom (2013)
8. Gürler, G., Görkemli, B., Saygili, G., Tekalp, A.M.: Flexible transport of 3-D video over networks. Proceedings of the IEEE 99(4), 694–707 (2011)
9. Leland, W.E., Taqqu, M.S., Willinger, W., Wilson, D.V.: On the self-similar nature of Ethernet traffic (extended version). IEEE/ACM Transactions on Networking 2(1), 1–15 (1994)
10. Melnikov, G., Katsaggelos, A.K.: A jointly optimal fractal/DCT compression scheme. IEEE Transactions on Multimedia 4(4), 413–422 (2002)
11. Merkle, P., Müller, K., Wiegand, T.: 3D video: acquisition, coding, and display. IEEE Transactions on Consumer Electronics 56(2), 946–950 (2010)
12. Morgade, J., Usandizaga, A., Angueira, P., de la Vega, D., Arrinda, A., Velez, M., Ordiales, J.: 3DTV roll-out scenarios: A DVB-T2 approach. IEEE Transactions on Broadcasting 57(2), 582–592 (2011)
13. Müller, K., Merkle, P., Tech, G., Wiegand, T.: 3D video formats and coding methods. In: Proceedings of the 17th IEEE International Conference on Image Processing (ICIP), Hong Kong, September 26-29 (2010)
14. Peitgen, H., Jürgens, H., Saupe, D.: Chaos and Fractals. Springer, New York (1992)
15. Pulipaka, A., Seeling, P., Reisslein, M., Karam, L.: Traffic and statistical multiplexing characterization of 3D video representation formats. IEEE Transactions on Broadcasting 59(2), 382–389 (2013)
16. Reljin, I., Samcovic, A., Reljin, B.: H.264/AVC video compressed traces: Multifractal and fractal analysis. EURASIP Journal on Advances in Signal Processing (2006)
17. Seeling, P., Fitzek, F.H.P., Reisslein, M.: Video Traces for Network Performance Evaluation. Springer, Dordrecht (2007)
18. Sheluhin, O., Smolskiy, S., Osin, A.: Self-Similar Processes in Telecommunications. John Wiley & Sons, Inc., New York (2007)
19. Smolic, A., Mueller, K., Merkle, P., Fehn, C., Käuff, P., Eisert, P., Wiegand, T.: 3D video and free viewpoint video - technologies, applications and MPEG standards. In: Proceedings of the IEEE International Conference on Multimedia and Expo, Toronto, July 9-12 (2006)
20. Taqqu, M., Teverovsky, V., Willinger, W.: Estimators for long-range dependence: an empirical study. Fractals 3(4), 785–798 (1995)
21. Vetro, A., Matusik, W., Pfister, H., Xin, J.: Coding approaches for end-to-end 3D TV systems. In: Proceedings of the Picture Coding Symposium (2004)
22. Vetro, A., Tourapis, A.M., Müller, K., Chen, T.: 3D-TV content storage and transmission. IEEE Transactions on Broadcasting 57(2), 384–394 (2011)

Adaptive Window Size Selection for Efficient Probability Estimation in Binary Range Coder of the 3-D DWT Video Codec

Evgeny Belyaev

Tampere University of Technology, Korkeakoulunkatu 10, 33720 Tampere, Finland
evgeny.belyaev@tut.fi

Abstract. In this paper we propose a new adaptive window size selection algorithm for efficient probability estimation in binary range coder. The proposed algorithm was embedded in low-complexity video codec based on three-dimensional discrete wavelet transform (3-D DWT). Simulation results show that for the basic 3-D DWT codec the proposed algorithm provides 0.2–1.2dB quality increase for a given bit rate at the price of the computational complexity increase from 1.4 to 2 times. Herewith, the modified 3-D DWT is from 1.6 to 5 times less complex for the same quality level compared to fast software implementation of the H.264/AVC standard (x264 codec in ultrafast mode). Therefore, it is more preferable than H.264/AVC if a low-complexity scalable video coding is needed.

Keywords: binary range coder, probability estimation, 3-D DWT.

Introduction

There exist video coding and transmission applications, such as video coding on mobile devices, video transmission for wireless sensor networks, wireless endoscope capsules, 3D videoconferencing and so on, in which video capturing, video encoding, decoding, packet loss protection and playback should operate in real-time and computational resources (or power consumption) for encoding are very restricted. At the same time, during transmission the video bit stream rate must be easily varied at the encoder side, and it should be easily truncated at any intermediate network node for adaptation to the channel bandwidth at the current link and or end-user display. It is well known that a low-complexity scalable video coding (SVC) is the most preferable compression method for such applications. However, the most popular SVC approach based on H.264/AVC standard [2] requires relatively a high computational resources which is a significant barrier for its use for these applications.

In our previous work [1] we have proposed a low-complexity scalable video coding algorithm based on three-dimensional discrete wavelet transform (3-D DWT). It was shown that the 3-D DWT video codec has a much lower computational complexity (from 2 to 6 times) compared to the H.264/AVC standard

M. Jonsson et al. (Eds.): MACOM 2014, LNCS 8715, pp. 112–120, 2014.

in the low complexity mode. However, in some cases, its rate-distortion performance can be lower than H.264/AVC (up to 2 dB). To improve the coding performance of the 3-D DWT codec, in this paper we propose a new adaptive virtual sliding window size selection algorithm for efficient probability estimation in binary range coder, which is a core part in wavelet subband bit-plane entropy encoder. We show that the modified 3-D DWT codec provides significant quality increase for a given bit rate. Herewith, its computational complexity is keeping less than the complexity of a fast software implementation of the H.264/AVC standard (x264 codec in ultrafast mode).

The rest of this paper is organized as follows. Section 1 describes the main idea of probability estimation based on virtual sliding window. Section 2 introduces a novel probability estimation algorithm using adaptive virtual sliding window size selection. The rate-distortion-complexity comparisons for the modified 3-D DWT codec, basic 3-D DWT codec from [1] and existing real-time software implementations of H.264/AVC standard are presented in Section 3. Finally, conclusions are drawn in Section 4.

1   Probability Estimation Using Virtual Sliding Window

One of the well known probability estimation algorithms is based on a sliding window concept. The probability of a source symbol is estimated by analyzing the content of a special buffer. This buffer keeps W previously encoded symbols, where W is the length of the buffer. After the encoding of each symbol the buffers content is shifted by one position, a new symbol is written to the free cell and the earliest symbol in the buffer is erased. The sliding window estimation can achieve a more accurate evaluation of the source statistics and a fast adaptation to the source statistics by increasing the window length W. However, the sliding window must be kept in the encoder and the decoder side, which can incur memory problem with an increasing size of W. In order to avoid memory usage, the following sliding window approximation called *virtual sliding window* was proposed in [3]. In this algorithm, the number of ones s_{t+1} in the window $W = 2^w$ after compression of binary symbol x_t is calculating by the following rule:

$$s_{t+1} = \begin{cases} s_t + \left\lfloor \dfrac{2^{2w} - s_t + 2^{w-1}}{2^w} \right\rfloor, & \text{if } x_t = 1 \\[4mm] s_t - \left\lfloor \dfrac{s_t + 2^{w-1}}{2^w} \right\rfloor, & \text{if } x_t = 0, \end{cases} \tag{1}$$

and the probability of ones is calculated as

$$\hat{p}_t = \frac{s_t}{2^{2w}}. \tag{2}$$

From (1) it follows that if the initial value s_0 satisfy

$$2^{w-1} - 1 \le s_0 \le 2^{2w} - 2^{w-1} + 1, \tag{3}$$

then during all operational time, the minimum possible state value is

$$s_{min}(w) = 2^{w-1} - 1. \tag{4}$$

2   Proposed Adaptive Window Size Selection

The virtual sliding window allows to easily control the trade-off between the speed of probability adaptation and the precision of probability estimation: small window lengths provide a fast adaptation to a new source statistics, but have low probability estimation precision, while longer windows provide better estimation precision, but have a slower adaptation speed. As a result, the best coding performance is achieved for a window which has a good balance of these two features. To achieve an even better compression performance we introduce the following *adaptive window size selection* algorithm. First, similarly to our previous work [5] we propose to use a high speed of probability adaptation at the initial stage of the coding using a small window lengths, and then, we propose to switch to a longer window length to provide a lower adaptation speed, but a better precision of the probability estimation. This approach is also adopted in the MQ-coder from JPEG2000 standard [7] utilizing three adaptation mechanisms, which are embedded into one state machine implemented by look-up tables.

Let use define as 2^{w_1} the initial window length, and s_1 as the corresponding state value. We encode the first n_1 symbols by window 2^{w_1}, and starting from symbol with index $n_1 + 1$ we use window $2^{w_2} > 2^{w_1}$ for the next n_2 symbols and so on, until the main window length 2^{w_m} is reached. Let us notice that following (2), each time, after encoding n_j symbols, we need to scale the state of window 2^{w_i} to the state of window 2^{w_j} as $s_j = s_i \cdot 2^{2(w_j - w_i)}$ to keep the same probability estimation value.

The main window length 2^{w_m} is used for the vast majority of encoded symbols. From (2) and (4) it follows, that using this window the probabilities in the interval $[\frac{2^{w_m-1}-1}{2^{2w_m}}, 0.5]$ can be estimated. However, in some cases the statistics of the binary source is such that the required probability estimation value belongs to the interval $[0, \frac{2^{w_m-1}-1}{2^{2w_m}})$ which cannot be reached by window 2^{w_m}. To overcome this problem we propose to use even longer window lengths for this interval of probabilities. If the current symbol is LPS (Least Probable Symbol) and $\left\lfloor \frac{s_m + 2^{w_m-1}}{2^{w_m}} \right\rfloor = 0$ (minimum possible probability estimation value for window 2^{w_m} is reached), we switch to window $2^{w_m+1} > 2^{w_m}$. If the current symbol is LPS and $\left\lfloor \frac{s_{m+1} + 2^{w_m+1-1}}{2^{w_m+1}} \right\rfloor = 0$, we switch to window $2^{w_m+2} > 2^{w_m+1}$ and so on, until the maximum window length is reached. Finally, if the current probability estimation is more than $\frac{2^{w_m-1}-1}{2^{2w_m}}$ then we switch back to the main window 2^{w_m}.

In this work the following window lengths are used: $W = \{2^3, 2^4, ..., 2^{10}\}$. Windows $W = 2^3$ and $W = 2^4$ are used at the initial stage of coding (see lines 17–22 in Algorithm 1). Taking into account that 16 LPS symbols for window $W = 2^3$ and 42 LPS symbols for $W = 2^4$ are enough to switch from the probability estimation value $\hat{p} = 0.5$ to the minimum possible probability estimation value, we set $n_1 = 16$ and $n_2 = 58$. Then the algorithm switches to window $W = 2^5$ (see lines 19–21 of Algorithm 1), which is used as the main window length, $w_m = 5$. Windows $W = 2^6, ..., 2^{10}$ are used for probability estimation in the interval $[0, \frac{1}{64})$. Lines 10–15 of Algorithm 1 perform the transition from window $W = 2^w$ to $W = 2^{w+1}$, while lines 6–8 of Algorithm 1 perform the switching back to the main window $W = 2^5$.

Algorithm 1. Proposed algorithm

1: **if** $x_t = $MPS **then**
2:      $s \leftarrow s + (2^{2w} - s + 2^{w-1}) \cdot 2^{-w}$
3:      **if** $s > 2^{2w-1}$ **then**
4:          MPS $\leftarrow$ 1$-$ MPS
5:          $s \leftarrow 2^{2w} - s$
6:      **else if** $w > w_m$ and $s > s_{min}(w_m) \cdot 2^{2(w-w_m)}$ **then**
7:          $s \leftarrow s \cdot 2^{-2(w-w_m)},\ w \leftarrow w_m$
8:      **end if**
9: **else**
10:      $\Delta s \leftarrow (s + 2^{w-1}) \cdot 2^{-w}$
11:      **if** $\Delta s = 0$ and $w \neq 10$ **then**
12:          $w \leftarrow w + 1,\ s \leftarrow 4s$
13:      **else**
14:          $s \leftarrow s - \Delta s$
15:      **end if**
16: **end if**
17: **if** $n = 16$ and $w = 3$ **then**
18:      $w \leftarrow w + 1,\ s \leftarrow 4s$
19: **end if**
20: **if** $n = 58$ and $w = 4$ **then**
21:      $w \leftarrow w + 1,\ s \leftarrow 4s$
22: **end if**
23: $n \leftarrow n + 1$

---

3   Simulation Results

Practical results were obtained for a high definition (1920 × 1080) test video sequences "ElFuente", "Pedestrian Area" and "Tractor" [10]. For our experiments, the binary range coder with the proposed adaptive window size selection was used in 3-D DWT codec [1] instead of initial combined entropy coder. The basic and modified codecs were run in constant bit rate mode with GOF size 16 using the Haar wavelet transform in the temporal direction and the 5/3 spatial lifting wavelet transform at three-levels of the decomposition. Tables 1–3 show Y-PSNR values for two codecs at the same target bit rate value. One can see, that the modified version of the codec provides 0.2–1.2dB quality increase for a given bit rate.

Table 1. Y-PSNR comparison for "ElFuente", dB

Target bit rate, kbps	3-D DWT [1]	Modified 3-D DWT
3000	37.76	38.41 (+0.64)
2000	36.18	36.60 (+0.42)
1000	32.87	33.46 (+0.59)
500	29.65	30.23 (+0.58)
250	25.99	27.06 (+1.07)

Table 2. Y-PSNR comparison for "Pedesrtian area", dB

Target bit rate, kbps	3-D DWT [1]	Modified 3-D DWT
6000	37.60	38.02 (+0.42)
3000	35.28	35.55 (+0.27)
2000	33.52	33.82 (+0.30)
1000	29.60	30.30 (+0.71)
500	24.80	25.99 (+1.19)

Table 3. Y-PSNR comparison for "Tractor", dB

Target bit rate, kbps	3-D DWT [1]	Modified 3-D DWT
14000	35.08	35.50 (+0.42)
7000	32.59	32.98 (+0.39)
3000	29.59	29.94 (+0.35)
2000	28.13	28.57 (+0.44)
1000	26.10	26.39 (+0.29)
500	24.30	24.69 (+0.39)

Additionally, we found that for a high definition video sequences the use of four-levels spatial decomposition can be much more efficient than three-levels decomposition. For example, at a low bit rates the quality increase can reach 1.5–3.5dB. Therefore, in our further experiments we use four-levels spatial decomposition in the modified version of the 3-D DWT codec.

The modified and basic 3-D DWT codecs were compared with the x.264 codec [8] which, as it is shown in [9] provides close to optimum rate-distortion performance for the H.264/AVC standard when computational complexity is significantly restricted. Therefore, this codec can be used as an upper bound of rate-distortion performance which can be achieved by H.264/AVC standard in a low complexity case. x.264 codec was run in very low complexity mode which corresponds to the Baseline profile of H.264/AVC with intra-frame period 16. The basic 3-D DWT codec was run with GOF size 16 using the Haar wavelet transform in the temporal direction and the 5/3 spatial lifting wavelet transform at three-levels of the decomposition. The modified 3-D DWT codec with the proposed adaptive window size selection algorithm was run with GOF size 16 using the Haar wavelet transform in the temporal direction and the 5/3 spatial

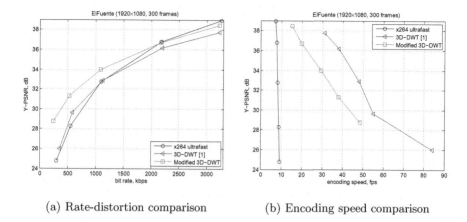

(a) Rate-distortion comparison   (b) Encoding speed comparison

Fig. 1. Rate-distortion-complexity comparison for ElFuente

a)   *b)*

Fig. 2. Visual comparison for ElFuente, $1920 \times 1080, 300$ frames, 500 kbps: a) x264 ultrafast, b) Modified 3-D DWT

lifting wavelet transform at four-levels of the decomposition. The constant bit rate mode was used in all cases.

Figures 1–6 show rate-distortion-complexity comparison as well as selected frames for visual assessment for the mentioned above codecs. The encoding speed in this paper is defined as the number of frames which can be encoded in one second on the hardware platform with processor Intel Core i3 CPU 2.1GHz and is measured without any use of assemblers, threads, or other program optimization techniques. The computational complexity is considered as inverse value of the encoding speed.

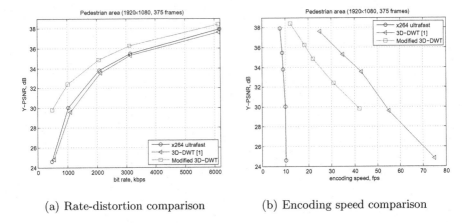

(a) Rate-distortion comparison   (b) Encoding speed comparison

Fig. 3. Rate-distortion-complexity comparison for Pedestrian area

Fig. 4. Visual comparison for Pedestrian area, $1920 \times 1080, 375$ frames, 500 kbps: a) x264 ultrafast, b) Proposed 3-D DWT

One can see that the modified 3-D DWT codec is up to 5dB better than the basic 3-D DWT codec proposed in [1], but at the price of increasing of the computational complexity from 1.4 to 2 times. Herewith, the modified 3-D DWT is from 1.6 to 5 times less complex for the same quality level compared to the fast software implementation of the H.264/AVC standard and provides much better objective and subjective visual quality at low bit rates (compare visual quality at Figures 2, 4 and 6).

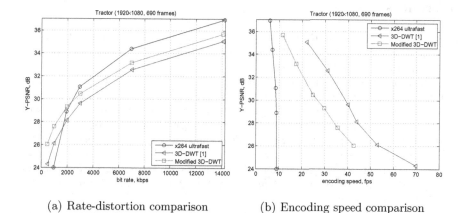

(a) Rate-distortion comparison   (b) Encoding speed comparison

Fig. 5. Rate-distortion-complexity comparison for Tractor

Fig. 6. Visual comparison for Tractor, $1920 \times 1080, 690$ frames, 500 kbps: a) x264 ultrafast, b) Proposed 3-D DWT

4   Conclusion

Taking into account that the proposed codec is able to generate a scalable video bit stream which is much more robust to packet losses than a stream generated by H.264/AVC standard [11], the modified 3-D DWT codec is more preferable than H.264/AVC in many applications in which the video encoding computational complexity or power consumption play a critical role.

References

1. Belyaev, E., Egiazarian, K., Gabbouj, M.: A low-complexity bit-plane entropy coding and rate control for 3-D DWT based video coding. IEEE Transactions on Multimedia 15(8), 1786–1799 (2013)
2. Advanced video coding for generic audiovisual services, ITU-T Recommendation H.264 and ISO/IEC 14496-10, AVC (2009)
3. Belyaev, E., Gilmutdinov, M., Turlikov, A.: Binary arithmetic coding system with adaptive probability estimation by Virtual Sliding Window. In: Proceedings of the 10th IEEE International Symposium on Consumer Electronics, pp. 194–198 (2006)
4. Belyaev, E., Veselov, A., Turlikov, A., Kai, L.: Complexity analysis of adaptive binary arithmetic coding software implementations. In: Balandin, S., Koucheryavy, Y., Hu, H. (eds.) NEW2AN 2011 and ruSMART 2011. LNCS, vol. 6869, pp. 598–607. Springer, Heidelberg (2011)
5. Belyaev, E., Turlikov, A., Egiazarian, K., Gabbouj, M.: An efficient adaptive binary arithmetic coder with low memory requirement. IEEE Journal of Selected Topics in Signal Processing. Special Issue on Video Coding: HEVC and Beyond 7(6), 1053–1061 (2013)
6. Belyaev, E.: Low bit rate video coding based on three-dimensional discrete pseudo cosine transform. In: International Conference on Ultra Modern Telecommunications (2010)
7. ITU-T and ISO/IEC JTC 1, JPEG 2000 Image Coding System: Core Coding System, ITU-T Recommendation T.800 and ISO/IEC 15444-1. JPEG 2000 (2000)
8. x.264 video codec, http://x264.nl/.
9. Li, X., Wien, M., Ohm, J.-R.: Rate-Complexity-Distortion Optimization for Hybrid Video Coding. IEEE Transactions on Circuits and Systems for Video Technology 21, 957–970 (2011)
10. Xiph.org test media, http://media.xiph.org/video/derf/
11. Belyaev, E., Egiazarian, K., Gabbouj, M., Liu, K.: A Low-complexity joint source-channel video coding for 3-D DWT codec. Journal of Communications 8(12) (2013)

Secret Communication When the Eavesdropper Might Be an Active Adversary

Andrey Garnaev and Wade Trappe

WINLAB, Rutgers University, North Brunswick, USA
garnaev@yahoo.com,
trappe@winlab.rutgers.edu

Abstract. We study how secret communication can be effected by the fact that an adversary's capability to eavesdrop on a collection of communications from a base station to a set of users may be restricted and unknown to the transmitter. In this situation, the eavesdropping adversary might have to choose which user to eavesdrop upon if it cannot eavesdrop upon the full set. Thus, the transmitter must make a decision on how to better maintain secret communication, and to do this it must take into account that the eavesdropper might possibly be passive or could be an active adversary that must actively make a choice about which user to eavesdrop upon. Using an example of a Bayesian game-theoretical model with unknown eavesdropping capacity we show why it is important to incorporate in a secret transmission protocol the possibility of an eavesdropper having restricted eavesdropping capacity. Also, since the equilibrium strategies are obtained explicitly, we establish some interesting properties that can guide deployment of such a system.

Keywords: Secret communication, Eavesdropping, Active eavesdropper, Bayesian game, Equilibrium strategies.

1 Introduction

The problem of establishing secret communication between a transmitter and a receiver is fundamental to building secure communication systems. The traditional approach to establishing confidential communications involves the use of cryptographic ciphers, i.e. algorithms that obfuscate (plaintext) information in such a way that adversaries who listen in on the obfuscated (ciphertext) information find it hard to infer the original plaintext information. Typically, the concept of *hard* is tied to there being an extreme *computational* advantage that the legitimate parties have over eavesdropping participants, and this notion of computational complexity underlying security serves as the basis for modern cryptography. An alternative formulation for secret communication is based on the notion of information-theoretic secrecy, where the adversary is assumed to have unlimited computational capabilities and the underlying issue is whether, under this assumption, an adversary can glean any information about the plaintext.

M. Jonsson et al. (Eds.): MACOM 2014, LNCS 8715, pp. 121–136, 2014.

Information-theoretic secrecy is founded on the original paper by Shannon [1], and received extensive attention in the context of the wiretap model by Wyner [2], the general broadcast scenario Csiszár and Körner [3], and in other settings by Maurer and Wolf [4]. More recently, the notion of information-theoretic secrecy has been applied to the problem of secret communication in wireless systems, and the reader is referred to [5, 6] for collections of papers that survey the field.

One of the fundamental approaches to achieving (or enhancing) secrecy that has come out of this research is to introduce interference into the medium so as to harm the eavesdropper's ability to eavesdrop while strengthening the ability for two legitimate entities to communicate [7]. Most of the research that has examined the use of interference to assist in secret communication has started from a simple adversarial model, where the adversary is not also empowered to use interference to their advantage. In other words, additional capabilities are given to the legitimate parties while the adversary is restricted to be purely a passive adversary. There has been another branch of research into using the diversity provided by multiple, parallel channels to support secret communication. For example, one can use parallel subchannels in combination with fading to achieve secret communication in OFDM-style (Orthogonal Frequency-Division Multiplexing) systems [8]. In all these works the eavesdropper was considered as a passive adversary. In [9] and [10], it was suggested to consider a more sophisticated adversary with the dual capability of either eavesdropping passively or jamming any ongoing transmission, also referred to as an active eavesdropper (in this paper, our use of active refers to the eavesdropper making an active choice of who to eavesdrop upon). In particular, this problem was investigated as a zero-sum game between the user and the sophisticated adversary. That approach was further developed in [11] for the case of many adversaries and the users communicating with others located outside of a secured zone. The adversaries and the users can choose channels to communicate or jam, but they cannot tune powers they employ. The problem was extended to the case in which the adversary, besides choosing a channel to attack can tune jamming power while the user adjusts the transmission power in OFDM [12] or CDMA (Code Division Multiple Access) networks [13].

In this paper, we suggest to consider the other type of the sophisticated adversary, who, due to restricted eavesdropping capacity has to choose which user to eavesdrop upon, while transmitter makes decision how better to maintain secrecy communication. Then, the eavesdropper turns from being passive to be an active adversary that makes a choice of which user to eavesdrop upon. By way of a Bayesian game-theoretical model with unknown eavesdropping capacity, we show how it is possible to deal with such a problem. Because equilibrium strategies are obtained explicitly, we obtain interesting properties and observations related to this scenario.

The organization of this paper is as follows: in Section 2, we first introduce the basic optimization model with passive eavesdropper. In Sections 3 and 4, we formulate and solve the game-theoretical model in general and for low SINR (Signal to Interference plus Noise Ratio) regimes, when the eavesdropper might be an active adversary. In Section 5, conclusions are presented. Finally, in Section 6, proofs of the results are offered.

2   Basic Optimization Model

Let us describe the basic optimization problem, which involves n users within a secure area communicating thorough a base station (BS). We portray this scenario in Figure 1(a). Each user employs a separate channel for communication, so that no signal interference occurs. The adversary intends to eavesdrop upon this communication. The BS, to maintain the secret communication of these users, has to allocate the total power $\bar{P}$ to the n users so as to minimize eavesdropping effectiveness (in some sense, BS solves a problem of fair allocation resource [14] with linear utilities of fairness among user to maintain secrecy communication). So, a strategy of the BS is a vector $\boldsymbol{P} = (P_1, \ldots, P_n)$ with P_i being the power assigned to the user i to transmit through channel i, $\sum_{i=1}^{n} P_i \leq \bar{P}$. The secrecy rate [11] of the user i is given by $CS = \ln(1 + h_i P_i) - \ln(1 + h_{Ei} P_i)$, where h_i is the fading main channel gains between ith communicating couple of the users, and h_{Ei} is the eavesdropping channel gains of these users. We assume in this work that eavesdropping channel gains are less than corresponding the main channel gains, i.e.

$$h_i \geq h_{Ei} \text{ for any } i. \tag{1}$$

In our optimization model in this section, we assume that the adversary has enough capability to eavesdrop upon all the channels (e.g. its RF front-end is capable of sampling a sufficiently wide bandwidth to capture all of the users). Thus, the payoff to the BS is the total secrecy capacity, i.e. it is given as follows:

$$v_B(\boldsymbol{P}) = \sum_{i=1}^{n} (\ln(1 + h_i P_i) - \ln(1 + h_{Ei} P_i)). \tag{2}$$

The BS wants to allocate power such way to maximize the total secrecy capacity, i.e. $\boldsymbol{P} = \arg_{\boldsymbol{P}} \max v_B(\boldsymbol{P})$. This problem can be solved using standard non-linear programming approach[15], namely, the following result holds.

Theorem 1. *The considered optimization problem of secrecy communication has the unique optimal solution $\boldsymbol{P}$, where*

$$P_i = \frac{1}{2h_i h_{Ei}} \left[\sqrt{(h_i - h_{Ei})^2 + 4h_i h_{Ei}(h_i - h_{Ei})/\omega} - h_i - h_{Ei} \right]_+ \text{ for } i \in [1, n], \tag{3}$$

where ω is the unique positive root of the following water-filling (it means that some of the channels to maintain secrecy due to water-filling nature of the optimizing strategy have to be excluded from communication):

$$\sum_{i=1}^{n} \frac{1}{2h_i h_{Ei}} \left[\sqrt{(h_i - h_{Ei})^2 + 4h_i h_{Ei}(h_i - h_{Ei})/\omega} - h_i - h_{Ei} \right]_+ = \bar{P}.$$

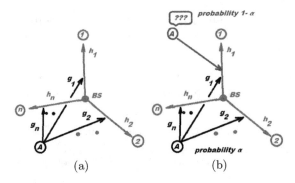

Fig. 1. (a) Relationships between base station, users and passive adversary, (b) Relationships between base station, users and adversary, when the adversary might be active

Figure 2(a) illustrates that the optimal BS payoff in the presence and absence of the adversary, as well as the adversary's payoff, are non-linear increasing functions of $\bar{P}$, where $n = 4$, $h_E = (0.1, 0.7, 1.1, 2.1)$ and $h = (1.1, 1.9, 2.5, 2.7)$ in this example. In the absence of the the adversary (so, when $h_{Ei} = 0$ for $i \in [1, n]$) the optimal power is $P_i^{abs} = [1/\omega - 1/h_i]_+$ for $i \in [1, n]$, where ω is the solution of the water-filling equation: $\sum_{i=1}^{n} [1/\omega - 1/h_i]_+ = \bar{P}$. Figure 2(b) illustrates the optimal BS strategies $P_i, i \in [1, 4]$ in the presence and $P_i^{abs}, i \in [1, 4]$ in the absence of the adversary. It is interesting that, due to relocating of the power resources caused by the potential eavesdropping, the relation between P_i and P_{iabs} can change to have an opposite behavior, for example, $P_2 > P_2^{abs}$ for small $\bar{P}$, and $P_2 < P_2^{abs}$ for big $\bar{P}$.

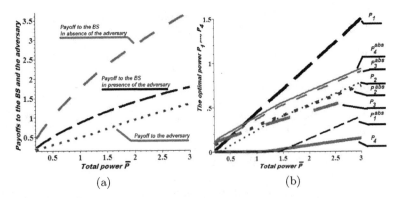

Fig. 2. (a) The optimal payoff to the BS in the presence and absence of the adversary as well as the adversary's payoff, (b) the BS optimal strategies $P_i, i \in [1, 4]$ in presence and $P_i^{abs}, i \in [1, 4]$ in absence of the adversary

3   Active Eavesdropper

In this section we consider the situation where the eavesdropping's technical characteristics might be such that it might have restricted eavesdropping capability, i.e. the adversary may not be able to eavesdrop on all of the channels at once. In this case the adversary turns from a passive adversary to an active one, since to eavesdrop effectively he must select which channels to eavesdrop upon. The BS does not know the eavesdropping capability of the adversary, and in this paper in order to get insight into the problem we consider that the restricted eavesdropping capacity is such that the adversary can only eavesdrop on one channel. This assumption will allow us to obtain explicit solutions and observe some interesting properties. Thus, we assume that the BS only knows that, with probability α, the adversary has the maximal eavesdropping capacity, i.e. he can eavesdrop on all the channels at once, or with probability $1 - \alpha$ he has the minimal one, i.e. the adversary can eavesdrop only on one channel (Figure 1(b)). In the last case, a strategy of the adversary is a probability vector $\boldsymbol{q} = (q_1, \ldots, q_n)$, where q_i is the probability to eavesdrop upon channel i. So, now the eavesdropper might be an active adversary making a decision of what channel to eavesdrop upon, and the BS does not know with certainty whether the eavesdropper is active or a passive adversary (capable of eavesdropping on all channels). The payoff to the BS is the expected secrecy rate given as follows:

$$
\begin{aligned}
v_B(\boldsymbol{P}, \boldsymbol{q}) = {} & \alpha \sum_{i=1}^{n} \left(\ln(1 + h_i P_i) - \ln(1 + h_{Ei} P_i) \right) \\
& + (1 - \alpha) \sum_{i=1}^{n} \left(\ln(1 + h_i P_i) - q_i \ln(1 + h_{Ei} P_i) \right).
\end{aligned}
\tag{4}
$$

The payoff to the adversary, with restricted capacity, is the expected eavesdropping secrecy rate reduction secrecy given as follows:

$$
v_A(\boldsymbol{P}, \boldsymbol{q}) = \sum_{i=1}^{n} q_i \ln(1 + h_{Ei} P_i),
\tag{5}
$$

and with un-restricted capacity:

$$
v_A(\boldsymbol{P}) = \sum_{i=1}^{n} \ln(1 + h_{Ei} P_i).
\tag{6}
$$

We will look for a (Bayesian) equilibrium, since the type (passive or active) of the eavesdropper is unknown to the BS, i.e. for a such pair of strategies $(\boldsymbol{P}, \boldsymbol{q})$ which are the best response strategies to each other, i.e.

$$
\boldsymbol{P} = \arg_{\boldsymbol{P}} \max v_B(\boldsymbol{P}, \boldsymbol{q}),
\tag{7}
$$

$$
\boldsymbol{q} = \arg_{\boldsymbol{q}} \max v_A(\boldsymbol{P}, \boldsymbol{q}).
\tag{8}
$$

Note that the Bayesian approach has been widely employed in dealing with different problems in networks, for example, intrusion detection [16–19] and transmission under incomplete information [20–26]. The following theorem supplies explicit solution of this problem.

Theorem 2. *The considered game has a unique equilibrium* $(\boldsymbol{P}, \boldsymbol{q})$, *where*

$$q_i = q_i(\omega, \nu) = \begin{cases} \dfrac{1}{(1-\alpha)h_{Ei}} \left(\dfrac{h_i h_{Ei} e^{\omega}}{h_i e^{\omega} + h_{Ei} - h_i} - \nu e^{\omega} - \alpha h_{Ei} \right), & i \in I_{11}(\omega, \nu), \\ 0, & i \notin I_{11}(\omega, \nu), \end{cases} \tag{9}$$

$$P_i = P_i(\omega, \nu) = \begin{cases} \dfrac{e^{\omega} - 1}{h_{Ei}}, & i \in I_{11}(\omega, \nu), \\ P_{10i}(\nu), & i \in I_{10}(\omega, \nu), \\ 0, & i \in I_{00}(\omega, \nu), \end{cases} \tag{10}$$

where

$$P_{10i}(\nu) := \frac{1-\alpha}{2\nu} - \frac{h_i + h_{Ei}}{2h_i h_{Ei}} \\ + \frac{\sqrt{\dfrac{((1-\alpha)h_i h_{Ei})^2}{\nu^2} + \dfrac{2(1+\alpha)h_i h_{Ei}(h_i - h_{Ei})}{\nu} + (h_i - h_{Ei})^2}}{2h_i h_{Ei}}, \tag{11}$$

$$I_{11}(\omega, \nu) := \{i : h_i - \alpha h_{Ei} > \nu, h_{Ei} P_{10i}(\nu) > e^{\omega} - 1\}, \tag{12}$$

$$I_{10}(\omega, \nu) := \{i : h_i - \alpha h_{Ei} > \nu, h_{Ei} P_{10i}(\nu) \leq e^{\omega} - 1\}, \tag{13}$$

$$I_{00}(\omega, \nu) := \{i : h_i - \alpha h_{Ei} \leq \nu\}. \tag{14}$$

The positive parameters ω *and* ν *are given unequally as follows:*

$$\nu = Y(x_*) \text{ and } \omega = x_*, \tag{15}$$

where for any fixed non-negative x, $Y = Y(x)$ *is the unique root of the following equation:*

$$\sum_{i=1}^{n} \frac{1}{(1-\alpha)h_{Ei}} \left[\frac{h_i h_{Ei} e^x}{h_i e^x + h_{Ei} - h_i} - Y e^x - \alpha h_{Ei} \right]_{+} = 1, \tag{16}$$

and x_* *is the unique root of the equation:*

$$\sum_{i \in I_{11}(x, Y(x))} \frac{1}{h_{Ei}} (e^x - 1) + \sum_{i \in I_{10}(x, Y(x))} P_{10i}(Y(x)) = \bar{P}. \tag{17}$$

Let us to illustrate the solution using a numerical example with $n = 5$ and channel gains $h_E = (0.4, 0.6, 1.1, 2.3, 2.6)$ and $h = (2.6, 2.9, 3.5, 4.4, 5.1)$. Figure 3 (a) illustrates that the payoffs to the BS's and passive adversary are decreasing continuous functions on the probability α, but the active adversary's payoff is a non-monotonic continuous function on the probability. So, the active adversary can gain from the expected threat to the *BS* from the passive adversary after a switching point (in this example that switching point is $\alpha = 0.89$). The *BS* employs all of the channels, while up until the switching point the active adversary uses two channels (4 and 5), and after the switching point he focuses on the only channel 5 (Figure 3 (b) and (c)). Figure 4(a) illustrates that the payoffs to the rivals are increasing with increasing total power. The *BS* can obtain it by monotonically increasing power in each channel, while the active adversary must use more sophisticated re-allocation effort, namely, he reduces probability of using channel 5 while increasing probability of using channel 4.

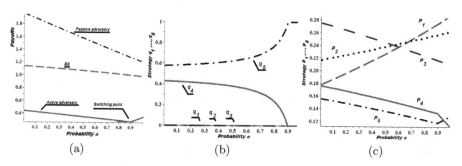

Fig. 3. (a) The payoffs to the *BS* and the adversary, (b) the adversary equilibrium strategy $q_i, i \in [1,5]$, (c) the *BS* equilibrium strategies $P_i, i \in [1,5]$ as functions of probability α

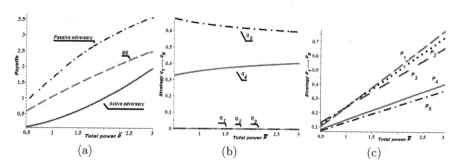

Fig. 4. (a) The payoffs to the *BS* and the adversary, (b) the adversary equilibrium strategy $q_i, i \in [1,5]$, (c) the *BS* equilibrium strategies $P_i, i \in [1,5]$ as functions of total power $\bar{P}$

4   Low SINR Regime

In the regime of low SINR, the Shannon capacity can be approximated by the signal to interference ratio (SINR). So, SINR can be considered as an objective function. A second motivation to consider SINR as the basis for an objective function (and not use Shannon capacity), is that current technology for voice over wireless does not try to achieve Shannon capacity but rather uses given codecs that can adapt the transmission rate to the SINR; these turn out to adapt the rate in a way that is linear in the SINR over a wide range of throughput. The SINR has thus been used very often to represent directly the throughput, see [27–31]. Thus, since in the low SINR regime $\ln(1 + \text{SINR}) \approx \text{SINR}$ for small enough SINR, the payoff to the BS turns into the following one:

$$
\begin{aligned}
v_B(\boldsymbol{P}, \boldsymbol{q}) &= \alpha \sum_{i=1}^{n} P_i(h_i - h_{Ei}) + (1 - \alpha) \sum_{i=1}^{n} P_i(h_i - q_i h_{Ei}) \\
&= \sum_{i=1}^{n} P_i(h_i - (\alpha + (1 - \alpha)q_i)h_{Ei}),
\end{aligned}
\tag{18}
$$

and the payoff to Eve is given as follows:

$$
v_A(\boldsymbol{P}, \boldsymbol{q}) = \sum_{i=1}^{n} P_i h_{Ei} q_i.
\tag{19}
$$

Without loss of generality, we can assume that the channels are arranged in increasing order by shifting gains around as follows:

$$
h_1 - \alpha h_{E1} \geq h_2 - \alpha h_{E2} \geq \ldots \geq h_n - \alpha h_{En}.
\tag{20}
$$

The following theorem shows that in the equilibrium behavior the adversary tries to eavesdrop only on the channels where it has better main channel gains, meanwhile the BS transmits its signal equalizing the expected damage from eavesdropping by taking into account only the spectrum used and the eavesdropper's channel gains. Also, the adversary equilibrium strategy is always unique, while the BS equilibrium strategy is unique except in a very particular situation, depending on the parameter of the network, when a continuum of the equilibrium can arise.

Theorem 3. *In the considered game for a low SINR regime there is a unique adversary's equilibrium strategy given as follows:*

$$
q_i = \begin{cases}
\dfrac{1}{1 - \alpha}\left(\dfrac{\displaystyle\sum_{j=1}^{k}((h_i - h_j)/h_{Ej}) + (k - 1)\alpha + 1}{\displaystyle\sum_{j=1}^{k}(h_{Ei}/h_{Ej})} - \alpha \right), & i \leq k, \\
0, & i > k + 1,
\end{cases}
\tag{21}
$$

where

$$
\varphi_k \leq 1 - \alpha < \varphi_{k+1}
\tag{22}
$$

and

$$
\varphi_m = \sum_{i=1}^{m}(h_i - h_m + \alpha(h_{Em} - h_{Ei}))/h_{Ei} \ \textit{for } m \in [1, n] \textit{ and } \varphi_{n+1} = \infty.
\tag{23}
$$

The BS equilibrium strategy is described in the following two subcases:
(i) If

$$v_k \neq h_k - \alpha h_{Ek}, \tag{24}$$

with

$$v_k = \frac{\displaystyle\sum_{i=1}^{k}(h_i/h_{Ei}) - (k-1)\alpha - 1}{\displaystyle\sum_{i=1}^{k}(1/h_{Ei})}, \tag{25}$$

then there is unique BS equilibrium strategy $\boldsymbol{P}$ given as follows:

$$P_i = \begin{cases} (1/h_{Ei})/(\sum_{j=1}^{k}(1/h_{Ej})), & i \leq k, \\ 0, & i \geq k+1. \end{cases} \tag{26}$$

(ii) If

$$v_k = h_k - \alpha h_{Ek}, \tag{27}$$

then there is a continuum of BS equilibrium strategies $\boldsymbol{P}$ given as follows:

$$P_i = \begin{cases} \nu/h_{Ei}, & i \in [1, k-1], \\ \nu\varepsilon_i, & i : h_i - \alpha h_{Ei} = h_k - \alpha h_{Ek}, \\ 0, & otherwise, \end{cases} \tag{28}$$

where $\varepsilon_i \leq 1/h_{Ei}$ for $i : h_i - \alpha h_{Ei} = h_k - \alpha h_{Ek}$ and

$$\nu = \bar{P}/\left(\sum_{j=1}^{k-1}(1/h_{Ej}) + \sum_{j:h_j-\alpha h_{Ej}=h_k-\alpha h_{Ek}} \varepsilon_j \right).$$

All these equilibrium strategies are equivalent to each other, since each of them return the same payoff.
The payoff to the BS is

$$v_B = v_k \bar{P}. \tag{29}$$

The BS equilibrium strategy equalizes the payoffs to passive and active types of the adversary making them equal to

$$v_A = \bar{P}/\left(\sum_{i=1}^{k}(1/h_{Ei}) \right). \tag{30}$$

It is interesting that the *BS* equilibrium strategy depends explicitly on the eavesdropping channel gains (26) and implicitly on the main channel gains (22) by means of the threshold channel k. Since the *BS* equilibrium depends explicitly only on the eavesdropping channel gains, it is quite natural that it has an equalizing eavesdropping capacity structure to maintain the same level of eavesdropped signal for each channel used for communication. If the eavesdropper is passive (so, $\alpha = 1$), then the optimal *BS* strategy is to transmit in channels

$i \in M_{BS}$, where $M_{BS} = \{i : i = \arg_i \max(h_i - h_{Ei})\}$. Of course, the channels $i = \arg_{i \in M_{BS}} \min h_{Ei}$ is preferable for use since it gives the minimal level of eavesdropping for maximum transmission secrecy capacity. Also, it is quite interesting that the set of channels chosen for transmission does not depend on the total power, and instead depends only on the main and eavesdropping channel gains.

Let us illustrate the solution using a numerical example with $\bar{P} = 1$, $h_E = (0.2, 1.1, 1.8, 2.3, 2.8)$ and $h = (1.6, 1.9, 2.5, 3, 3.2)$. Figure 5(a) illustrates that the BS's payoff is a decreasing continuous piecewise linear function on the probability α (see (29)), but the adversary's payoff is a non-monotonic discontinuous piecewise constant function (see (30)) on the probability. In the sense of continuity, the equilibrium strategies exchange their roles: the adversary's strategy is a discontinuous function of the probability α, but the BS's strategy is a continuous function on the probability α (5(b) and (c)). It is interesting that the number of used channels is not monotonous on the probability α. For $\alpha \in (0, 0.4)$ three channels $\{3, 4, 5\}$ are in use, for $\alpha \in (0.4, 0.6)$ four channels $\{1, 3, 4, 5\}$ are in use, for $\alpha \in (0.6, 0.65)$ again three channels $\{1, 4, 5\}$ are in use, for $\alpha \in (0.65, 0.7)$ two channels $\{1, 4\}$ are in use, and finally for $\alpha \in (0.7, 1)$ the only channel 1 is in use. The channel 2 is not used at all for any α, so $q_2 = P_2 = 0$.

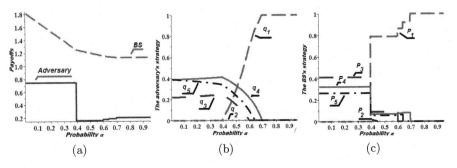

Fig. 5. (a) The payoffs to the BS and the adversary, (b) the adversary equilibrium strategy $q_i, i \in [1, 5]$, (c) the BS equilibrium strategies $P_i, i \in [1, 5]$ as functions on probability α

5   Conclusions

To get insight into the problem of how secret communication can be effected by the fact that the adversary's eavesdropping ability might be restricted and unknown to a transmitter, we have formulated and explicitly solved a Bayesian game-theoretical model of this problem. We have shown that, in designing a secret transmission protocol, is important to incorporate information about the adversary's eavesdropping capability even if there is the potential that adversary has restricted ability to eavesdrop. We have shown by properly choosing the channels to eavesdrop upon, such an adversary can gain due to the "double

possible threat" for secret transmission arising from the possibility that the
adversary may be either passive or an active type of adversary. We have shown
that, in the general SINR regime, there are unique equilibrium strategies, while
in the low SINR regime a continuum of the adversary equilibrium strategies can
arise. Also, in the low SINR regime the adversary strategy becomes very sensitive
to the parameters of the networks, namely, for general SINR his strategy is
continuous while for low SINR regime it can have jump discontinuities. Finally
note, that a goal of our future work is to investigate more general the adversary's
eavesdropping capability.

References

1. Shannon, C.E.: Communication theory of secrecy systems. Bell Syst. Tech. J. 28, 656–715 (1949)
2. Wyner, A.D.: The wire-tap channel. Bell Syst. Tech. J. 54, 1355–1387 (1975)
3. Csiszar, I., Korner, J.: Broadcast channels with confidential messages. IEEE Trans. Inform. Theory 24, 339–348 (1978)
4. Maurer, U.M., Wolf, S.: Information-theoretic key agreement: From weak to strong secrecy for free. In: Preneel, B. (ed.) EUROCRYPT 2000. LNCS, vol. 1807, pp. 351–368. Springer, Heidelberg (2000)
5. Liang, Y., Poor, H.V., Shamai, S.: Information Theoretic Security. Now Publishers, MA (2009)
6. Bloch, M., Barros, J.: Physical Layer Security. Cambridge University Press, Cambridge (2011)
7. Koyluoglu, O.O., El Gamal, H., Lai, L., Poor, H.V.: Interference alignment for secrecy. IEEE Trans. Inform. Theory 57, 3323–3332 (2011)
8. Li, Z., Yates, R., Trappe, W.: Secrecy capacity of independent parallel channels. In: Securing Wireless Communications at the Physical Layer, pp. 1–18. Springer (2010)
9. Amariucai, G.T.: Physical security in wireless networks: intelligent jamming and eavesdropping. PhD thesis, Louisiana State University, USA (2009)
10. Mukherjee, A., Swindlehurst, A.L.: Optimal strategies for countering dual-threat jamming/eavesdropping-capable adversaries in MIMO channels. In: Proceedings of MILCOM 2010, pp. 1695–1700 (2010)
11. Zhu, Q., Saad, W., Han, Z., Poor, H.V., Basar, T.: Eavesdropping and jamming in next-generation wireless networks: a game-theoretic approach. In: Proceedings of MILCOM 2011, pp. 119–124 (2011)
12. Garnaev, A., Trappe, W.: The eavesdropping and jamming dilemma in multi-channel communications. In: Proceedings of 2013 IEEE International Conference on Communications (ICC), pp. 753–757 (2013)
13. Garnaev, A., Trappe, W.: To eavesdrop or jam, that is the question. In: Sherif, M.H., et al. (eds.) ADHOCNETS 2013. LNICST, vol. 129, pp. 146–161. Springer, Heidelberg (2014)
14. Altman, E., Avrachenkov, K., Garnaev, A.: Generalized α-fair resource allocation in wireless networks. In: Proceedings of 47th IEEE Conference on Decision and Control (CDC 2008), pp. 2414–2419 (2008)
15. Gopala, P.K., Lai, L., El Gamal, H.: On the secrecy capacity of fading channels. IEEE Trans. Inform. Theory 54, 4687–4698 (2008)

16. Liu, Y., Comaniciu, C., Mani, H.: A Bayesian game approach for intrusion detection in wireless ad hoc networks. In: Proceedings of Valuetools 2006 (2006)

17. Agah, A., Das, S.K., Basu, K., Asadi, M.: A Bayesian game approach for intrusion detection in wireless Ad Hoc networks. In: Proceedings of the 3rd IEEE International Symposium on Network Computing and Applications (NCA), pp. 243–346 (2004)

18. Garnaev, A., Trappe, W., Kung, C.-T.: Dependence of optimal monitoring strategy on the application to be protected. In: Proceedings of 2012 IEEE Global Communications Conference (GLOBECOM), pp. 1054–1059 (2012)

19. Garnaev, A., Baykal-Gursoy, M., Poor, H.V.: Incorporating attack-type uncertainty into network protection. IEEE Transactions on Information Forensics and Security 9, 1278–1287 (2014), doi:10.1109/TIFS.2014.2329241

20. Han, Z., Marina, N., Debbah, M., Hjrungnes, A.: Physical layer security game: Interaction between source, eavesdropper, and friendly jammer. EURASIP Journal on Wireless Communications and Networking (2009), Article ID 452907

21. Altman, E., Avrachenkov, K., Garnaev, A.: Fair resource allocation in wireless networks in the presence of a jammer. Performance Evaluation 67, 338–349 (2010)

22. He, G., Debbah, M., Altman, E.: κ-player Bayesian waterfilling game for fading multiple access channels. In: Proceedings of the 3rd IEEE International Workshop on Computational Advances in Multi-Sensor Adaptive Processing (CAMSAP), pp. 17–20 (2009)

23. Heikkinen, T.: A minmax game of power control in a wireless network under incomplete information. Technical Report 99–43, DIMACS, New Brunswick, NJ (1999)

24. Jean, S., Jabbari, B.: Bayesian game-theoretic modeling of transmit power determination in a self-organizing CDMA wireless network. In: Proceedings of 60th IEEE Vehicular Technology Conference (VTC), vol. 5, pp. 3496–3500 (2004)

25. Adlakha, S., Johari, R., Goldsmith, A.: Competition in wireless systems via bayesian inference games (2007), http://arxiv.org/abs/0709.0516

26. Garnaev, A., Hayel, Y., Altman, E.: A Bayesian jamming game in an OFDM wireless network. In: Proceedings of 2012 10th International Symposium on Modeling and Optimization in Mobile, Ad Hoc and Wireless Networks (WIOPT), pp. 41–48 (2012)

27. Kim, S.L., Rosberg, Z., Zander, J.: Combined power control and transmission rate selection in cellular networks. In: Proceedings of IEEE VTC 1999, vol. 3, pp. 1653–1657 (1999)

28. Koo, I., Ahn, J., Lee, H.A., Kim, K.: Analysis of erlang capacity for the multimedia DS-CDMA systems. IEICE Trans. Fundamentals E82-A, 849–855 (1999)

29. Altman, E., Avrachenkov, K., Garnaev, A.: Transmission power control game with SINR as objective function. In: Altman, E., Chaintreau, A. (eds.) NET-COOP 2008. LNCS, vol. 5425, pp. 112–120. Springer, Heidelberg (2009)

30. Yang, D., Zhang, J., Fang, X., Xue, G.: Optimal transmission power control in the presence of a smart jammer. In: Proceedings of IEEE Global Communications Conference (GLOBECOM), pp. 5506–5511 (2012)

31. Altman, E., Avrachenkov, K., Garnaev, A.: Jamming in wireless networks under uncertainty. Mobile Networks and Applications 16, 246–254 (2011)

32. Fudenberg, D., Tirole, J.: Game theory. MIT Press, Boston (1991)

6   Appendix

6.1   Proof of Theorem 2

Since v_B is concave on $\boldsymbol{P}$ and v_A is linear on $\boldsymbol{q}$, the game has an equilibrium [32]. To find the equilibrium, recall that a couple of strategies $(\boldsymbol{P}, \boldsymbol{q})$ is an equilibrium if and only if the strategies are the best response to each other, so (7) and (8) hold. Since v_B is concave on $\boldsymbol{P}$, then by Kuhn-Tucker theorem of non-linear programming $\boldsymbol{P}$ is the best response strategy to $\boldsymbol{q}$ if and only if there is ν (Lagrangian multiplier) such that

$$\frac{h_i}{1 + h_i P_i} - \frac{(\alpha + (1-\alpha)q_i)h_{Ei}}{1 + h_{Ei}P_i} \begin{cases} = \nu, & P_i > 0, \\ \leq \nu, & P_i = 0. \end{cases} \tag{31}$$

Since v_A is linear on $\boldsymbol{q}$, $\boldsymbol{q}$ is the best response to $\boldsymbol{P}$ if and only if there is ω (maximal coefficient of $\boldsymbol{q}$) such that

$$\ln(1 + h_{Ei}P_i) \begin{cases} = \omega, & q_i > 0, \\ \leq \omega, & q_i = 0. \end{cases} \tag{32}$$

First, we will find P_i and q_i given by (31) and (32) implicitly as functions on ω and ν. Namely, we will prove that they have to have the form given by (9) and (10).

Let, for a while, ω and ν be fixed. Note that, by (32), if $P_i = 0$ then $q_i = 0$. So, there is no i such that $q_i > 0$ and $P_i = 0$, what is quite natural since there is no sense eavesdropping channels unused for transmission.

Let $I_{11} = \{i : P_i > 0, q_i > 0\}$, $I_{10} = \{i : P_i > 0, q_i = 0\}$ and $I_{00} = \{i : P_i = 0, q_i = 0\}$. Consider separately three cases: (i) $i \in I_{00}$, (ii) $i \in I_{10}$ and (iii) $i \in I_{11}$.

(i) Let $i \in I_{00}$. By (31) and (32), $I_{00} = I_{00}(\nu, \omega)$ with $I_{00}(\nu, \omega)$ given by (14).

(ii) Let $i \in I_{10}$. Then, by (31) and (32),

$$\frac{h_i}{1 + h_i P_i} - \frac{\alpha h_{Ei}}{1 + h_{Ei}P_i} = \nu, \tag{33}$$

and

$$\ln(1 + h_{Ei}P_i) \leq \omega. \tag{34}$$

By the assumption (1), left side of equation (33) is decreasing on P_i from $h_i - \alpha h_{Ei}$ for $P_i = 0$ to zero for $P_i \uparrow \infty$. So, it has a positive root if and only if

$$h_i - \alpha h_{Ei} > \nu, \tag{35}$$

and this root is unique, and it is $P_i = P_{10i}(\nu)$, where $P_{10i}(\nu)$ is given by (11).

Note that, $P_{10i}(\nu)$ is decreasing on ν. Then, by (34) and (35), $I_{10} = I_{10}(\omega, \nu)$, where $I_{10}(\omega, \nu)$ is given by (13).

(iii) Let $i \in I_{11}$. Then, by (31) and (32),

$$h_i/(1 + h_i P_i) - (\alpha + (1-\alpha)q_i)h_{Ei}/(1 + h_{Ei}P_i) = \nu \tag{36}$$

and

$$\ln(1 + h_{Ei}P_i) = \omega. \tag{37}$$

By (37),

$$P_i = P_i(\omega) := (e^\omega - 1)/h_{Ei}. \tag{38}$$

Substituting this P_i into (36) yields

$$q_i = q_i(\omega, \nu) = \frac{1}{(1-\alpha)h_{Ei}} \left(\frac{h_i h_{Ei} e^\omega}{h_i e^\omega + h_{Ei} - h_i} - \nu e^\omega - \alpha h_{Ei} \right). \tag{39}$$

By (36) P_i is decreasing on q_i, thus, by (33), (34), (36) and (37) we have that $I_{11} = I_{11}(\omega, \nu)$, where $I_{11}(\omega, \nu)$ is given by (12).

Then, results of (i)-(iii) imply that $P_i = P_i(\omega, \nu)$ and $q_i = q_i(\omega, \nu)$ has to have the form given by (9) and (10). We will find ω and ν that $\boldsymbol{P}$ is a vector of allocation of total power $\bar{P}$ and $\boldsymbol{q}$ is a probability vector, i.e. ω and ν have to be solution of the following two nonlinear equations:

$$Q(\omega, \nu) := \sum_{i=1}^n q_i(\omega, \nu) = 1, \tag{40}$$

$$P(\omega, \nu) := \sum_{i=1}^n P_i(\omega, \nu) = \bar{P}. \tag{41}$$

By (9) and (14), $Q(\omega, \nu)$ has the following properties:

(Q_1) Q is continuous on ω and ν,
(Q_2) Q is decreasing on ω and ν.

Also,

$$Q(\omega, 0) = \sum_{i=1}^n \frac{1}{1-\alpha} \left[\frac{h_i e^\omega}{h_i e^\omega + h_{Ei} - h_i} - \alpha \right]_+ > (\text{by } (Q_2)) > \lim_{\omega \uparrow \infty} Q(\omega, 0) = n > 1,$$

and

$$Q(\omega, \bar{h}) = 0, \text{ where } \bar{h} = \max_i (h_i - \alpha h_{Ei}).$$

So, for any fixed ω there is $\nu = Y(\omega) \in (0, \bar{h})$ such that

$$Q(\omega, Y(\omega)) = 1.$$

By (9), this equation coincides with (16). Also, by properties (Q_1) and (Q_2), Y has the following properties:

(Y_1) Y is continuous on ω,
(Y_2) Y is decreasing on ω from $Y(0)$ for $\omega = 0$ to zero for $\omega \uparrow \infty$.

Substituting $\nu = Y(\omega)$ into (41) we obtain the equation only for variable ω.

$$P(\omega, Y(\omega)) = \bar{P}. \tag{42}$$

By (10), this equation coincides with (17). Also, by (10), $P(\omega, \nu)$ is continuous function on ω and ν, it is increasing on ω and decreasing on ν. Thus, by properties (Y_1) and (Y_2), $P(\omega, Y(\omega))$ is increasing function on ω from zero for $\omega \downarrow 0$ to infinity for $\omega \uparrow \infty$. Thus, equation (42) has the unique root, and the result follows. ∎

6.2   Proof of Theorem 3

Since v_B is linear on $\boldsymbol{P}$, and v_A is linear on $\boldsymbol{q}$, then the equilibrium exists [32]. Equilibrium strategies $\boldsymbol{P}$ and $\boldsymbol{q}$ are the best response to each other. Thus, due to linearity of the payoffs, $(\boldsymbol{P}, \boldsymbol{q})$ is an equilibrium if and only if there are ω (the maximal coefficient of $\boldsymbol{P}$ in v_B) and ν (the maximal coefficient of $\boldsymbol{q}$ in v_A) such that

$$h_i - (\alpha + (1-\alpha)q_i)h_{Ei} \begin{cases} = \omega, & P_i > 0, \\ \leq \omega, & P_i = 0, \end{cases} \tag{43}$$

$$h_{Ei}P_i \begin{cases} = \nu, & q_i > 0, \\ \leq \nu, & q_i = 0. \end{cases} \tag{44}$$

By (44), if $P_i = 0$ then $q_i = 0$. Let $I_{00}^L = \{i : P_i = 0, q_i = 0\}$, $I_{10}^L = \{i : P_i > 0, q_i = 0\}$ and $I_{11}^L = \{i : P_i > 0, q_i > 0\}$. By (43), $I_{00}^L = \{i : h_i - \alpha h_{Ei} \leq \omega\}$.

Let $i \in I_{11}^L$. Then, by (43) and (44),

$$h_i - (\alpha + (1-\alpha)q_i)h_{Ei} = \omega, \tag{45}$$
$$h_{Ei}P_i = \nu. \tag{46}$$

So,

$$P_i = \nu/h_{Ei} \tag{47}$$

and

$$q_i = ((h_i - \omega)/h_{Ei} - \alpha)/(1-\alpha). \tag{48}$$

Thus, by (48), $I_{11}^L = I_{11}^L(\omega) := \{i : h_i - \alpha h_{Ei} > \omega\}$.

Let $i \in I_{10}^L$. Then, by (43) and (44),

$$h_i - \alpha + h_{Ei} = \omega, \tag{49}$$

$$P_i \leq \nu/h_{Ei}. \tag{50}$$

Then, by (48), we have that ω is an unique root of the equation

$$\sum_{i=1}^{n} [(h_i - \omega)/h_{Ei} - \alpha]_+ /(1-\alpha) = 1, \tag{51}$$

and the equilibrium strategy $\boldsymbol{q}$ is uniquely

$$q_i = [(h_i - \omega)/h_{Ei} - \alpha]_+ /(1-\alpha) \text{ for } i \in [1, n], \tag{52}$$

with ω given by (51). If there is no k such that $h_k - \alpha h_{Ek} = \omega$, then (49), $I_{10}^L = \emptyset$. Then, by (47), P also is uniquely defined as follows,

$$P_i = \begin{cases} (1/h_{Ei}) / \left(\sum_{j \in I_{11}^L(\omega)} (1/h_{Ej}) \right), & i \in I_{11}^L(\omega), \\ 0, & i \notin I_{11}^L(\omega). \end{cases} \tag{53}$$

If there is a k such that $h_k - \alpha h_{Ek} = \omega$, then (49), $I_{10}^L = \{i : h_i - \alpha h_{Ei}\}$ and q is uniquely defined with such ω. By (47), P is given as follows,

$$P_i = \begin{cases} \nu/h_{Ei}, & i \in I_{11}^L(\omega), \\ \leq \nu/h_{Ei}, & i \in I_{10}^L(\omega), \\ 0, & i \in I_{00}^L(\omega). \end{cases} \tag{54}$$

Thus, there are continuum of P, namely, all such P are given as follows:

$$P_i = \begin{cases} \nu/h_{Ei}, & i \in I_{11}^L(\omega), \\ \nu\varepsilon_i, & i \in I_{10}^L(\omega), \\ 0, & i \in I_{00}^L(\omega), \end{cases} \tag{55}$$

where $\varepsilon_i \leq 1/h_{Ei}$ for $i \in I_{10}^L(\omega)$ and $\nu = \bar{P} / \left(\sum_{j \in I_{11}^L(\omega)} (1/h_{Ej}) + \sum_{j \in I_{11}^L(\omega)} \varepsilon_j \right)$.

Taking into account the assumption (20) we can present solution in explicit form. By (20) and (52), there is a k such that

$$q_i = \begin{cases} \dfrac{1}{1-\alpha} \left(\dfrac{h_i - \omega}{h_{Ei}} - \alpha \right), & i \in [1, k], \\ 0, & i \in [k+1, n]. \end{cases} \tag{56}$$

Summing up (56) and taking into account that q is a probability vector yields:

$$\omega = v_k \tag{57}$$

with v_k given by (25). Also, by (52) and (56), k is such that: $(h_k - \omega)/h_{Ek} - \alpha \geq 0 > (h_{k+1} - \omega)/h_{E(k+1)} - \alpha$. Then, (56) and (57) imply that k is unique defined by the inequalities (22) with φ_i given by (23). Since φ_i is increasing, such k is unique defined, and the result follows. ∎

Author Index